# Workbook

Robert McLarty

**B1** >

# Business Partner

# Contents

# 1 Career choices

**Vocabulary** | Transferable skills

**1** Complete these comments by interviewers using the words and phrases in the box.

> can-do attitude   communication skills   critical thinking   determination
> integrity   set goals   team player   think outside the box

1 His ideas were creative and really innovative so he can obviously _____ .

2 I liked the way she worked with the other candidates so she is clearly a(n) _____ .

3 He has excellent _____ . The presentation was first class and he answered the questions really clearly.

4 She used _____ brilliantly. I thought she evaluated the three options in the case study carefully before deciding which one to choose.

5 She has a lot of _____ . This is the third time she's applied for a position in Marketing so she hasn't stopped trying.

6 I like the way she has monthly objectives for herself which shows she can _____ .

7 I don't think he will complain about work. He seems prepared to try anything. He has a real _____ .

8 They all seemed to have _____ . They answered the interview questions on attitudes towards work very well.

**2** Choose the correct option in italics.

1 Our consultants need to be *confident / independent* because they often have to work alone.

2 My manager is really *ambitious / passionate* about customer service.

3 In an interview you need to show *adaptability / confidence* in your abilities.

4 After four years in the job her *motivation / passion* was quite low and she started to look for a new one.

5 Our budgets are not high so we need to be very *resourceful / ambitious* when planning travel.

6 We get lots of different projects in our company so staff have to show great *adaptability / authenticity*.

**3** Complete the sentences using the correct word ending.

1 Juan can deal with most people and all the managers trust him – he is very depend_____ .

2 Things change so often in our industry. We have to be very flex_____ .

3 Anna really enjoys working on her own from home. She shows great independ_____ .

4 Henri loves his job and is really keen. It's good to see such enthus_____ .

5 My manager is always really hon_____ with me. He always tells me what he thinks.

6 Maria wants to become a manager in the next two years – she has a lot of amb_____ .

## Grammar  Advice and suggestions

**1** Complete the table using the problems and advice/suggestions in the box.

> How about looking for a new one?  I don't find my job very challenging.
> I've got too many online connections.  It takes me two hours to get to work.
> Why don't you go travelling until then?  You ought to go on a course.
> You should try thinking about something completely different.

| | Problem | Advice/Suggestion |
|---|---|---|
| 1 | My computer skills are not very good. | |
| 2 | | Why not try speaking to your manager? |
| 3 | I really don't earn enough in my present job. | |
| 4 | | You shouldn't accept everybody. |
| 5 | My new job starts in three months. | |
| 6 | | You could apply for a transfer to another branch. |
| 7 | I get so nervous before interviews. | |

**2** Match 1–7 with a–g to complete the sentences.

1 Why don't you
2 How about asking
3 You should always
4 You could do
5 You shouldn't
6 Why not try
7 You ought

a keep your profile updated.
b contacting a recruitment agency?
c get a better photo for your online profile?
d put false information on your profile.
e to rewrite your introduction.
f people to endorse your profile?
g some online courses to improve your CV.

**3** Put the dialogue in the correct order (1–8). Two lines have been done for you.

a How's it going?  _1_

b Why don't you apply for a working visa for Australia or New Zealand?  ___

c I haven't got enough money. Those courses are expensive.  ___

d I tried that but no luck. They said I need to improve my English.  ___

e Not too bad but I'm still looking for a job.  ___

f That's a good idea. I could get a job and learn English at the same time.  _8_

g You could go on an intensive course.  ___

h How about contacting a recruitment agency?  ___

## Reading

● ● ●   www.jobspot.abc

# The fun is over
## Work starts now

A lot of people ask me about the difference between studying and working full-time. Well, let me tell you it is very different. When you're studying, you set your goals and do enough studying to achieve them. Usually you like the subject, so most tasks are interesting. Once you start working though, someone else is managing you, setting your goals and making sure you achieve them. And, if you do, you can be sure they'll make them more difficult the next month!

Another important difference is that when you start work you often have no one below you. Even if you are the best in your class, graduating cum laude* in your subject, you probably have little practical experience in the workplace, so you start at the bottom. And some of the tasks you have to do will be very boring, so it's important you can motivate yourself. In sales, for example, they will often ask you to call old customers. You'll need determination, because you might call many of them without getting any interest, but you still have to be friendly and polite. I know this doesn't sound great but with a can-do attitude you can really start to make progress.

If you get a job in a non-customer facing position, you'll need to be able to work independently. You might be inputting data or preparing reports. Both of these tasks are necessary for your employer but might seem rather dull to you. Nevertheless, you'll need to be both reliable and a problem-solver, while finding the most efficient ways of doing them. Nobody said that work was always exciting!

And for those graduates who are still looking for a job, remember that you are competing with a lot of people every time you apply for a position; you need to make sure your online profile is up-to-date and makes you stand out from the crowd**. Why not try doing some online courses to improve your skills set and to give yourself something different to offer? You should always remember to be flexible. The job you're offered might not be exactly what you're looking for but it's only the first step on a long road.

*cum laude /kʊm ˈlaʊdeɪ/ (with honours) – if you graduate cum laude, you finish a university degree and are given official praise for special achievement

** stand out from the crowd – to be noticed because you are better than others

**1** Read the blogpost and decide if these statements are *true* (T), *false* (F) or *doesn't say* (DS).

1 You set your own goals when you're studying and when you start working.   ___

2 The best graduates might manage people in their first job.   ___

3 Subject knowledge is important in sales.   ___

4 Graduates in non-customer facing jobs need to be good at solving problems.   ___

5 Candidates with much better online profiles usually get the jobs they apply for.   ___

6 Graduates looking for work should consider additional studying.   ___

**2** Read the blogpost again and complete the sentences using the words and phrases in the box.

| at the bottom   can-do attitude   determined   harder   sets the goals   stand out |
| --- |

1 One main difference between studying and working is that at work another person _____ .

2 If you achieve your goals, the next ones will be _____ .

3 Graduates probably have to begin their career _____ .

4 You need to be _____ if the task takes a lot of time and is boring.

5 A(n) _____ is useful if you want to make progress.

6 The writer thinks you need to _____ from other candidates for a job.

**3** What is the best description of the blogpost?

a honest       b unrealistic       c positive

## Functional language

### Asking questions to build rapport

**1** Put the words in the correct order to make follow-up questions.

**A:** I hear you speak fluent English. Where did you learn it?

**B:** My parents worked in the UK. We lived in a town called Abingdon. [1]_____ ? (it / you / do / know)

**A:** Yes, I do actually. I studied near there for two years at the European School.

**B:** Really? Me too. [2]_____ ? (in / Abingdon / how / for / long / were / you)

**A:** Three years. From 2012 to 2014. [3]_____ ? (stay / long / how / you / did)

**B:** From 2008 to 2012. My mother worked in Oxford.

**A:** My father worked there, too. [4]_____ ? (live / exactly / where / you / did)

**B:** We lived in a small village called Burcot. Then we moved to London.

**A:** That's interesting. [5]_____ ? (there / do / what / you / did)

**B:** I went to university. Did you like England? [6]_____ ? (visit / which / you / places / did)

**A:** London, Bath and parts of Scotland.

**B:** [7]_____ ? (it / what / about / you / did / like)

**A:** I loved everything – the green hills, the grand buildings and all my friends!

**B:** Me, too. I miss it now!

### Networking at a careers event

**2** Which of these answers is not an appropriate response?

1 Starting a conversation: 'Sorry, could I just ask you a few questions about your company?'

  **a** Sure, go ahead.   **b** Oh, really?   **c** Yes, of course.

2 Showing interest: 'After college, I went to Salamanca to study Economics.'

  **a** That's interesting.   **b** Uh-huh.   **c** Here's my card.

3 Closing a conversation: 'Enjoy the rest of the event.'

  **a** I really appreciate your time, thank you.   **b** That sounds exciting.   **c** It's been nice talking to you.

**3** Complete the conversations using the words in the box.

> appreciate   call   detail   exciting   explain   minute   questions

**1 A:** Can I talk to you for a _____ ?
**B:** Of course, how can I help?

**2 A:** Thank you for your time. I really _____ it.
**B:** Thank you, too. It was a pleasure talking to you.

**3 A:** I've got some great news about our sales!
**B:** Have you? That sounds _____ .

**4 A:** I'd like to ask you a few _____ .
**B:** Sure. Go ahead.

**5 A:** Do you have a few minutes to _____ your new service?
**B:** Absolutely.

**6 A:** We need to discuss the report in more _____ .
**B:** We do. Could I give you a(n) _____ this afternoon?

## Writing    Emails – Introducing yourself

**1A**  **Read the two emails. Which is less formal?**

---

**To:** Sales consultants

**From:** Harry Kaufmann

**Subject:** Hello!

¹_____ colleagues,

²_____ as the new Social Media Communications Manager. Before I joined this company, I was working in a similar position for a German company. I have always wanted to work in Australia, so I am delighted to have this opportunity.

³_____ to contact me by email or phone if you have any questions. ⁴_____ meeting you all in person over the next few weeks.

⁵_____ ,

Harry Kaufmann

---

**To:** Marketing team

**From:** Emily Jones

**Subject:** Morning!

Hi everyone,

⁶_____ I want to introduce myself to you. I've just started work here to do maternity cover for Sally Jackson for the next six months. I'll be working mainly on social media projects. ⁷_____ receptionist before, so I am really excited about the change. ⁸_____ over lunch today. Or call me or message me if you want to meet up for coffee.

⁹_____ ,

Emily

---

**B**  **Read the emails again and complete them using the phrases in the box.**

| Best wishes    Dear    I very much look forward to    I was a    I would like to introduce myself |
| I'm Emily Jones and    Please feel free    Kind regards    Perhaps we can meet up |

**2**  **Brite a short email of about 80 words introducing yourself to your new classmates or colleagues.**

- Decide whether to write a formal or informal email.

- Begin and end appropriately.

- Introduce yourself.

- Say what you were doing previously.

- Offer the chance to meet people.

## Vocabulary  Sectors and industries

**1** Correct the underlined word in each sentence.

1 The tertiary ~~industry~~ *sector* includes education, public transport and financial services among others.

2 The <u>transportation</u> industry is a difficult sector at the moment as fewer people are buying new cars.

3 I work in <u>manufacturing</u>. I manage a large supermarket outside Warsaw.

4 The largest part of the Australian economy is the <u>automotive</u> sector, with tourism growing year on year.

5 The <u>oil</u> industry is in decline in our country because it is cheaper to make goods abroad.

6 With so many goods moving around the world, companies in <u>fishing</u> have great opportunities.

**2** Complete the sentences using the words and phrases in the box.

agriculture  construction  cruise ships  health care
insurance  metal extraction  oil drilling  raw materials

1 One of Saudi Arabia's key industrial activities is _____ and refining.

2 France is still very economically dependent on _____ so its farmers are very important.

3 Australia has developed efficient techniques for _____ which means the raw material can be mined quickly.

4 Croatia has expanded two of its ports so_____ can include them in their itineraries.

5 A big problem for this century will be _____ for older people who are living longer.

6 Brazil exports _____ to China who use them for manufacturing.

7 In Qatar, the _____ industry is expanding as they continue to need new hotels and malls.

8 The financial sector in the UK continues to grow, particularly _____ as companies need to cover their commercial risks.

**3** Choose the odd one out. Then match groups 1–6 to categories a–f.

| | a | b | c | d |
|---|---|---|---|---|
| 1 | hotel chain | airline | bank | campsite |
| 2 | coal mining | wine producing | gas extraction | oil drilling |
| 3 | car plant | steel factory | furniture maker | farm |
| 4 | book shop | factory | supermarket | restaurant |
| 5 | metal extraction | fishing | robotics | agriculture |
| 6 | chemical plant | insurance company | credit card company | bank |

a finance ___          d manufacturing ___

b retail ___            e raw material extraction ___

c primary sector ___    f tourism ___

## Grammar  Past Simple and Past Continuous

**1** Put the dialogue in the correct order (1–8). Two lines have been done for you.

**a** Why were you late? What happened? ___

**b** What were you doing last night? You look tired!  _1_

**c** Really? How do you know him? ___

**d** So you had dinner together? ___

**e** Yes, we did. And another old friend phoned while we were eating, so she came along, too!  _8_

**f** Well. We were looking at the menu when an old colleague, Gaspare, came in. ___

**g** I met him while I was working in Rome. ___

**h** We went out to an Italian restaurant for an early dinner but in the end, we stayed very late. ___

**2** Complete the sentences using the correct form of the words in the box.

check   discuss   give   go   have   join   talk   work

**1** While I _____ to a colleague, my mobile rang.

**2** My manager called me and _____ me some important news.

**3** When I _____ the company, only four other people were working there.

**4** I _____ for a competitor in Tokyo when I first met my boss.

**5** While she was giving her presentation, the lights suddenly _____ out.

**6** I _____ a brilliant idea while I was driving to work today.

**7** I got to the meeting late and when I arrived my colleagues _____ the budget.

**8** First, I _____ my email and then I made some calls.

**3** Choose the correct option in italics.

Some days are good but today was just perfect. ¹*When / While* I woke up, the sun was shining. I got up and I ²*had / was having* a shower when my phone rang. It was my boss. ³*When / While* he was talking, I got a message from a customer. She wanted to see me as soon as possible, so while I ⁴*listened / was listening* to my boss, I quickly got dressed and got in my car. While I ⁵*drove / was driving* to see the customer, I heard on the radio about a competition to win a holiday. When I parked at the customer's office, I ⁶*sent / was sending* a text to enter the competition. ⁷*While / When* I was waiting for the customer, I got a message on my phone. My customer arrived at that moment and we started the meeting, so I didn't have time to actually read the message. The customer had good news for us – a big order. We were discussing the details when my boss ⁸*called back / was calling back*. He ⁹*wanted / was wanting* to offer me a promotion! When I arrived at my office, I ¹⁰*saw / was seeing* the text from earlier which said I was the winner of the competition. What a day!

Onshore wind farm

**Listening**  **1**  🔊 2.01  **Listen to a podcast about business and the environment. Choose the correct option in italics.**

1  The discussion is about the use of *wind / waves* as a source of energy.

2  The wind farm in New Zealand is *on the land / in the sea*.

3  The industry is becoming more *expensive / economical*.

4  There is *a lot of / not much* wind in New Zealand.

5  Electricity is now *cheaper / more expensive* than it was.

6  Modern turbines stop turning if the wind is over *14 kph / 90 kph*.

**2**  **Listen again and decide if the statements are *true* (T) or *false* (F).**

1  John Preston's company manages wind farms on land.  ___

2  The wind farm and the farm in New Zealand are on the same land.  ___

3  Wind power is renewable.  ___

4  The turbines are often inactive.  ___

5  Americans are interested in onshore and offshore wind farms.  ___

6  Fossil fuels are now more necessary than ever.  ___

**3**  **Complete the notes. Then listen again and check your answers.**

## Wind farms

Wind is an important source of [1]_____ .

Wind farms can be offshore or [2]_____ .

A number of energy [3]_____ are starting to look at wind power.

Wind power works best in a(n) [4]_____ country.

[5]_____ is improving every year.

Turbines stop working when the wind is too [6]_____ .

UK companies have projects in the USA, [7]_____ and Germany.

**Functional language**

## Interrupting and dealing with interruptions

**1** Complete the phrases using the words in the box. There is one extra word.

| ahead as continue excuse finish interrupt just making say saying something speak thing |
|---|

**1** Please go _____ .

**2** Sure, please _____ .

**3** Going back to what I was _____ ...

**4** Sorry to _____ .

**5** So, _____ I was saying, ...

**6** _____ me for interrupting.

**7** Sorry, I just have one more _____ to say.

**8** What did you want to _____ ?

**9** Can I just say _____ here?

**10** The point I was _____ was ...

**11** Can I just _____ my point?

**12** Before you _____ , let me just say ...

## Leaving a voicemail message

**2A** 🔊 2.02 Listen to the voicemail and complete the message.

| | | |
|---|---|---|
| **Caller:**<br>Morgane [1]_____ | **Date/Time:**<br>19.7.17 / 10.20 | **Message for:**<br>Julio Casas in the [2]_____ |

**Reason for call:**
Discuss order [3]_____

**Please call back on:**
[4]08_____

**Comments:**
If unavailable organise another [5]_____ by email

**Action:**
Return the call by [6]_____ tomorrow.

**B** Complete the phrases Morgane used in her voicemail. Then listen again and check your answers.

| | Morgane |
|---|---|
| **Identify** | [1]_____ Morgane ... I'll [2]_____ that for you ... |
| **State the reason for the call** | [3]_____ for Julio Casas.<br>You asked me to [4]_____ you to discuss ... |
| **Request action** | [5]_____ call me back on my [6]_____ ? |
| **Leave details** | In case you don't have [7]_____ , I'm on ... |
| **Offer an alternative communication mode** | Can you [8]_____ me an email so we can fix ... |
| **Provide a deadline** | Could you [9]_____ me by ... ? |
| **Finish the call** | I [10]_____ to hearing from you. |

## Writing   Emails – Action points

**1A**  🔊 2.03  Listen to the end of a meeting and complete the email below.

---

**To:** All team members

**From:** Leona Walsh

**Subject:** Marketing

Dear all,

Thanks again for coming to the meeting yesterday. As you know, we are planning to launch a new advertising campaign for our domestic range in September this year. At our meeting, we planned the next steps starting from next week. As you can see, we have a lot to do. Here are the **key action points**.

|  | WHO | WHEN |
|---|---|---|
| Discussion of new [1]_____ | Leona | July 1st |
| Plan new [2]_____ | Jack | [3]_____ |
| [4]_____ social media | [5]_____ | August 15th |
| [6]_____ for launch event | Kathy | [7]_____ |
| [8]_____ guests to launch event | [9]_____ | [10]_____ |

Kind regards,

Leona

---

**B**  Look at these tips about action points. Which ones does Leona get right?

1  Give brief background about the meeting which led to the action points.

2  List the points in the order in which you must do them.

3  Use the same grammatical structure at the beginning of every action point.

4  Add the name of the person who is going to do the task if possible.

5  Put the date you want the task finished if possible.

**2**  Use the notes from the management meeting to write a short email with action points of about 100 words.

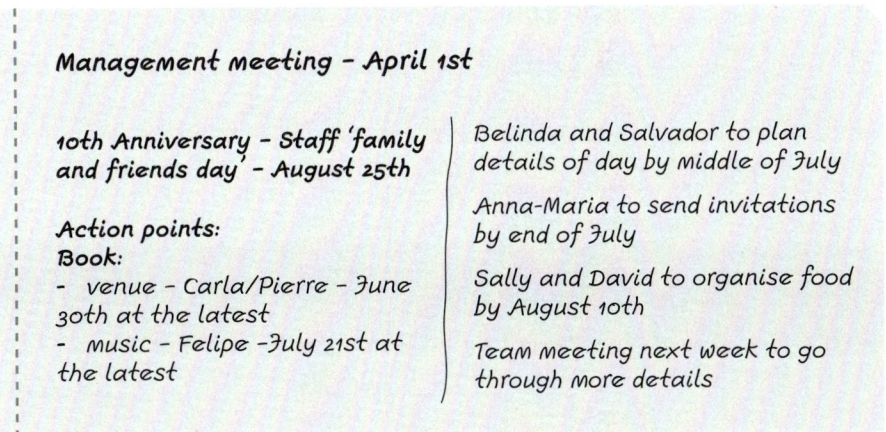

*Management meeting – April 1st*

*10th Anniversary – Staff 'family and friends day' – August 25th*

*Action points:*
*Book:*
*- venue – Carla/Pierre – June 30th at the latest*
*- music – Felipe – July 21st at the latest*

*Belinda and Salvador to plan details of day by middle of July*

*Anna-Maria to send invitations by end of July*

*Sally and David to organise food by August 10th*

*Team meeting next week to go through more details*

- Begin and end the email appropriately.
- Follow the tips in Exercise 1B.
- Make sure you include all the items in the notes.

# 3 > Projects

**Vocabulary**

## Managing projects

**1** Match the questions (1–6) with the responses (a–f).

1 So, Judith, how is the project going?

2 Setback? What happened?

3 How much longer?

4 So have we gone over budget?

5 Well done. What about the schedule?

6 And what is the deadline for materials to arrive?

**a** Four days. We anticipated finishing on Tuesday, not Saturday.

**b** Mid July is the final deadline. Construction starts on the 20th.

**c** Phase 2 took longer than we predicted.

**d** Very well, although we had one setback last week.

**e** The next milestone is the end of Phase 4 at the end of the month.

**f** Yes, we have, but we can save money on Phase 3.

**2** Choose the correct option in italics.

Home > Manage > Top 5 Project Management Tips

## Top 5 Project Management Tips

1 Make sure that your *schedule / management* is realistic and that everyone agrees to the dates.

2 *Manage / Anticipate* problems and plan solutions.

3 Have *risk / milestones* at various points on the schedule and arrange meetings for those times.

4 Never go over *management / budget*.

5 *Milestones / Setbacks* will happen so try to learn from them.

6 Spend time on *people / risk* management and check you have thought about all possibilities.

7 Keep a risk *diary / register* and add any new ones which occur.

8 As project *manager / budget*, make sure you have a good project team.

## Word building – verbs and nouns

**3** Complete the sentences using the correct form of the words in the box.

| add attach construct identify investigate manage move solve |

1 With more and more building in city centres, the _____ industry continues to grow.

2 I am delighted to announce a(n) _____ to our project team. His name is James Martin.

3 Please find my CV as a(n) _____ to this email.

4 The project was delayed while we _____ a gas leak.

5 In the end, the only _____ was to demolish two of the old buildings.

6 Security is strict at the site, so please bring proof of _____ .

7 We have some really large equipment for _____ tonnes of earth really quickly.

8 The success of the project was due to good _____ .

## Grammar Comparatives and superlatives

**1** Read the text and complete the sentences using the comparative, superlative or base form of the adjectives in the box.

# Three amazing bridges
## Three ambitious tourist attractions

In 2015, work started on Germany's longest suspension bridge in Geierlay and it opened five months later, one of the fastest bridge constructions ever. It is 400 m long and the drop down to the canyon below is nearly 100 m. Around 170,000 tourists per year are expected to use it and see the most spectacular views. The bridge is made of steel and cost around $1 million but extra tourism revenue in the area should be worth around $2 million. In China, the Zhangjiajie Glass Bridge opened a year later in 2016. This is the highest and longest glass-bottomed bridge in the world. Its length is 430 m and from the bridge you can look down 300 m to the canyon below.

At a cost of $2.6 million, it is made from the toughest glass available and attracts a lot of thrill–seeking tourists. It really is one of the scariest destinations in the region. The bridge can hold 800 people at the same time in complete safety! Meanwhile, one of the oldest pedestrian bridges in the world can be found in British Columbia, Canada, over the Capilano River. Built in 1889 by a Scottish engineer using rope and wood, the bridge is 150 m long and is suspended 80 m above the river. Tourists can cross the river and then walk on other bridges between the giant firs of the Capilano Forest, some of the biggest trees in Canada.

> most amazing    expensive    higher    longer    scariest
> most spectacular    tallest    most amazing

**1** The Capilano Bridge is by far the _____ of the three dating back to the 19th century.

**2** The Geierlay Bridge cost around $1 million, so it wasn't as _____ as the Glass Bridge.

**3** At 300 m, the Glass Bridge is much _____ than the other two.

**4** The Geierlay Bridge is _____ than the Capilano Bridge but shorter than the Glass Bridge.

**5** From all three bridges you get some of the _____ views in the world.

**6** The author thinks the Glass Bridge is one of the _____ places to visit.

**7** The trees in the Capilano Forest are among the _____ trees in North America.

**8** All three bridges are some of the _____ tourist attractions in the world.

**2** Correct the underlined words using the comparative, superlative or base form of the adjectives.

**1** People say that the Armani Hotel, built in Dubai in 2010, is the ~~more beautiful~~ *most beautiful* hotel in the world, with gold tablets in the bedrooms!

**2** Seven of the world's ten <u>busy</u> ports are in China – and Shanghai holds the number 1 position.

**3** The single span suspension bridge in Japan, which measures nearly 4,000 m, is <u>long</u> than any other in the world.

**4** At 632 m, the Shanghai Tower isn't as <u>higher</u> as the 828 m Burj Khalifa in Dubai.

**5** The Abraj Al-Bait in Mecca is the world's <u>more expensive</u> building, costing $15 billion.

**6** The Abraj Al-Bait hotel has the world's <u>big</u> clock which can be seen from 30 km away.

**7** The <u>heavy</u> cruise ship ever built is the *Symphony of the Seas*, weighing 230,000 tonnes.

**8** The Channel Tunnel was one of the <u>complex</u> engineering projects ever attempted but it was a complete success.

## Reading

# Crossrail crosses London

The £14.8 billion Crossrail project remains Europe's largest infrastructure project to date. Construction started in 2009 with a plan to build a modern railway line going across London from east to west that also connected with London's underground network. The Tube, as this network is known, was started in 1863 and is the world's oldest underground train system; it carries huge numbers every day in quite crowded conditions.

The Crossrail project added 42 km of tunnels, built ten new stations, modernised another thirty stations and created links to the existing transport system. The new state-of-the-art trains are much longer than the normal underground trains and are able to carry 1,500 passengers at a time. In total, London's rail capacity increased by 10 percent. This has encouraged more people to take public transport instead of driving and has helped to reduce pollution in the capital. Because the new trains are much faster than the old ones, an extra 1.5 million people are within 45 minutes of central London. The new line can carry 200 million passengers a year not only more quickly, but also in more comfortable surroundings.

The idea for a railway crossing London was first discussed over a hundred years ago and then again in the 1970s, but it was only in the new century that London decided to go ahead with this massive engineering project.

According to the company that ran the project, everything was completed on time and within budget. The project provided work for 55,000 people and offered 75,000 business opportunities to suppliers. The new line opened in 2018 and is called the Elizabeth line. It links Heathrow and Reading to the capital. Although those living in and close to London see the benefits of this project, people in other parts of the UK are not so happy. They feel that London continues to grow and offer the best jobs and highest salaries, while the rest of the country falls behind and feels poorer.

**1** Read the article and complete the table with the correct numbers.

| | | | | | |
|---|---|---|---|---|---|
| 1 | Cost of project | | 6 | Length of new tunnels | |
| 2 | Start of work | | 7 | Capacity of new trains | |
| 3 | Opening | | 8 | Increase in rail capacity | |
| 4 | Maximum journey time to central London | | 9 | Jobs created | |
| 5 | Annual passenger capacity | | 10 | Business opportunities | |

**2** Read the article again and choose the correct option.

1 Crossrail was a project which built

   **a** a new railway system to replace the Tube.

   **b** a new tube line to replace the railway.

   **c** a train line crossing London which links to the Tube.

2 The London Tube is

   **a** very comfortable and up to date.

   **b** usually quite empty.

   **c** the oldest underground railway in the world.

3 The Crossrail project involved

   **a** building 40 new stations.

   **b** modernising old tunnels.

   **c** building new tunnels and stations.

4 The green benefit of the project is that

   **a** the lines are underground, not overground.

   **b** more people might take public transport instead of using their cars.

   **c** the new trains are state-of-the-art.

5 The original idea for a railway crossing London

   **a** was discussed over a century ago.

   **b** was Queen Elizabeth's.

   **c** was thought about in the 1970s.

6 Although there are lots of benefits for London,

   **a** people from outside London have quite negative feelings.

   **b** people in other regions have better salaries.

   **c** the city is getting smaller.

### Functional language

## Giving and responding to instructions, standing your ground

**1** Complete the conversations between a manager (Anna) and two of her team (Marco and Sylvia) using the phrases in the box.

> bring me up to speed    can certainly do that    can't compromise    leave it with me
> my hands are tied    no room for manoeuvre    you need to meet

**Conversation 1**

**A:** How's the Dutch project going, Marco? Can you ¹_____ ?

**M:** It's going well but I don't think we have enough people to meet the deadline.

**A:** But you have a team of six. Surely that's enough?

**M:** Well, two of them are very inexperienced and another has been working part-time on another project.

**A:** I'm sorry, Marco but I have ²_____ on this. We told the customer the price based on a team of six for eight weeks.

**M:** In that case, can I exchange Charlie for someone like Giulia who has more experience? I know it might be difficult, Anna, but I ³_____ on this. I need more experience on the team. I'll make the deadline but I need Giulia.

**A:** OK. I'll arrange it.

**Conversation 2**

**A:** Come in, Sylvia. I need some help from you and your team. The customer called and asked if we could finish the project ten days earlier. What do you think?

**S:** Well ... I think we can finish a week earlier but ten days is a lot to ask.

**A:** ⁴_____ . I'm sorry. The Sales Director has now agreed on June 7th.

**S:** Can you give me any extra people?

**A:** Yes, I ⁵_____ . How about Charlie from Marco's team?

**S:** Is that OK with Marco?

**A:** ⁶_____ this new deadline. I'm sure he'll say yes.

**S:** So, I can definitely have the extra person?

**A:** No problem, ⁷_____ .

## Asking for and giving updates

**2** Choose the correct option in italics to complete the team meeting.

**A:** Thanks for coming both of you. It's good to catch up. How are we ¹ *meeting / doing* with the Dutch project, Marco?

**M:** Well, George is working full-time on another project this week and Charlie is really finding it hard. We expect to be trying out the prototype next week. What's ² *doing / happening* with Giulia's transfer?

**A:** Good news. She can start next week on a part-time basis and go full-time from the week after. What's the ³ *progress / latest* on the schedule?

**M:** We are OK to meet the deadline but everyone is working extra hours.

**S:** Same here! ⁴ *Where / Why* are we with Charlie's situation? Is he moving to my team?

**A:** Yes, next week. Sylvia, can you give me a(n) ⁵ *draft / update* on the testing phase?

**S:** Yes, my plan is to ⁶ *finish / agree* creating the new schedule later today and confirm that we can test from June 1st to 6th. It's tight but it fits in with the new deadline. The only ⁷ *impediment / programme* I see now is staffing. But it's always like that, isn't it?

**A:** It is. Thanks for the updates. I'll ⁸ *follow / close* up on the staff requests later.

## Writing  Email requesting an update

**1** Complete the email using the expressions in the box.

a  Could you let me know

b  I need your help with

c  I'd appreciate it if you could

d  I'd like to know if

e  Would it be possible to

f  Would you mind

---

**To:**  Clara Newman

**From:**  Claudia Gomez

**Subject:**  Update

Dear Clara,

I hope you are well. It was good to catch up with you last week at the training course. I'm writing because ¹_____ the monthly report. I know you're busy but it's important. ²_____ what the current position is?
³_____ the first phase of the project is now complete. If not, what date do you have for completion? And is Dieter now working on the project? ⁴_____ give me his starting date. ⁵_____ sending me final figures for the project? Sorry to ask so many questions. ⁶_____ have this information by tomorrow? I'd also like to request a meeting with the customer in Rome next week. I'd therefore be grateful if you could contact him and arrange it. I think that's all.

Kind regards,

Claudia

---

**2** Write an email of about 150 words asking for a project update using the notes below.

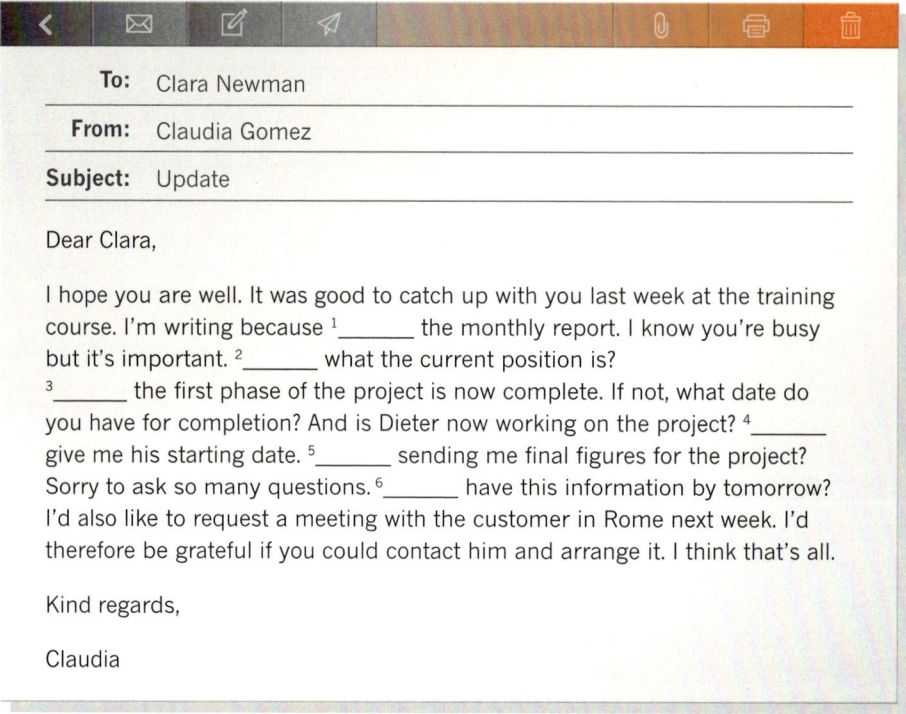

*Email to Jason about China project*

- *thank him for catch up last Thursday at project meeting*
- *need help with presentation to HR next week*
- *Is third phase complete? (if 'no' – completion date?)*
- *Is Emilia working? (starting date?)*
- *send latest schedule – tomorrow if possible!*
- *arrange meeting with customer in April in Hong Kong*

- Begin and end the email appropriately.

- Use a variety of statements and questions in your email to get the information you require.

- Make sure you include all the items in the notes.

# 4 > Global markets

**Vocabulary** **Global markets: Adjective and noun collocations**

**1 Complete the collocations. The first letters are given.**

1 Our new Marketing Director changed our m __ __ k __ __ __ __ __ g  st __ __ __ __ __ y to include more use of social media.

2 Most car companies allow you to choose from many options when buying a new car and this pr __ __ __ __ t  c __ st __ __ __ __  sa __ __ __ n is very popular with customers.

3 We have to alter our products to suit our tar __ __ t  t __ __ __ __ __ __ __ __ ies because there are different things to consider for each market.

4 The world's largest co __ __ __ __ __ er  br __ __ ds are often associated with global sports events, such as the Olympic Games.

5 Food companies such as PepsiCo have to think about l __ __ __ l  pr __ f __ __ __ __ ces when deciding which flavours to promote in a particular region.

6 Many brands of lu __ __ __ y  g __ __ ds have outlets at large international airports targeting the wealthy traveller.

## Global markets: Word building

**2 Choose the correct option in italics.**

1 The Mini is definitely my favourite car ever! I *prefer / preferable* it to all the others on the market.

2 The Mini is *produced / product* in the UK and the Netherlands.

3 So many other cars are *standard / standardise* these days but my Mini is unique.

4 When I was ordering it, I could choose all my *preferable / preferences* online.

5 In fact, there are so many options for the *customisation / customisable* of a Mini that they say there are 10 million different combinations!

6 It's really *adaptation / adaptable*, too, so I can use it to go to work, pick up the children or go on holiday.

**3 Complete the text using the correct form of the words in the box.**

| appeal   consume   customise   grow   produce   specialise   target |

### A unique car — for everyone

One of the most [1]_____ cars in the world, the Mini, is loved by [2]_____ everywhere. The main [3]_____ plant is in Oxford, UK where around 170,000 cars are made. Since 2001, over 3,000,000 have left the factory and most of them are [4]_____ for the person buying it. The Oxford plant [5]_____ in robotics with over 1,000 robots working on the production line. The [6]_____ in sales means that the parent company, BMW, is now making the car in the Netherlands as well, and they are using innovative advertising to [7]_____ even more potential new customers.

## Grammar    Present Simple and Past Simple passive

**1** Complete the sentences using the active or passive form of the verb in the Present Simple or Past Simple.

1 Our new website _____ (launch) last month and it has been very successful.

2 Stella McCartney _____ (run) her own fashion house.

3 The Dutch plant _____ (build) in just over twelve months and opened in May.

4 Hundreds of aircraft _____ (make) by Boeing every year.

5 They _____ (recommend) contacting them by email, but I never got a reply.

6 When they arrived at the hotel, they _____ (give) the wrong room.

7 During the storm, all flights to New York _____ (divert) to Washington.

8 It _____ (think) that there are more phones than people in the world.

**2** Read the text and complete the sentences using the correct form of the verbs in the box. Use both active and passive forms of the Present Simple or Past Simple.

In 1996, Geert-Jan Bruinsma had the idea of connecting hotels and guests via the internet and founded a small company with this aim. From an office in Amsterdam he developed a website called Bookings.nl and for the next few years the company experienced steady growth. The growth was noticed by an American company now called Booking Holdings Inc., who acquired them in 2006 for just over $130 million. Priceline kept the original management team and let them continue to develop the product. They were merged with another Priceline subsidiary called Active Hotels later the same year. Until then, most hotels got customers through travel agents but the arrival of this new business model changed travel for ever. Since then, Booking.com™ has become an internet phenomenon. It is said to be the largest advertiser on Google and is known as one of the easiest and most reliable websites in the world. Its webpages are translated into over 40 different languages and users book around a million room nights daily through the platform.

| book   buy   connect   found   grow   merge   say   translate |

1 With Booking.com, hotels and guests _____ via the internet.

2 The original company _____ in Amsterdam in 1996.

3 Over the next few years, sales _____ steadily.

4 The company _____ by The Priceline Group in 2006 for just over $130 million.

5 The two subsidiaries, Active Hotels and Bookings.nl _____ by Priceline in 2006.

6 People _____ that Booking.com is the largest advertiser on Google.

7 Booking.com currently _____ its webpages into over 40 different languages.

8 Around a million room nights _____ every day.

**3** Complete the questions and answers.

1 **A:** When _____ ?
   **B:** The company was founded in 1996.

2 **A:** How did the business grow for the next few years?
   **B:** It _____ steadily.

3 **A:** Who _____ by in 2006?
   **B:** They were bought by The Priceline Group.

4 **A:** How much did Priceline pay for Booking.com?
   **B:** They _____ just over $130 million.

5 **A:** Who _____ with?
   **B:** They were merged with Active Hotels.

6 **A:** How many languages _____ into?
   **B:** Its webpages are translated into over 40 languages.

**Listening** **1** 🔊 4.01 **Listen to a presentation and choose the correct option.**

**1** Who is giving the presentation?

    **a** a student

    **b** a competitor

    **c** an employee of the company

**2** What is the subject of the presentation?

    **a** a fast-food restaurant chain

    **b** a brand of crisps

    **c** a brand of drink

**2** **Listen again and decide if these statements are *true* (T) or *false* (F).**

**1** 'Chips' and 'crisps' sometimes mean the same thing. ___

**2** The speaker talks about social media as part of a marketing strategy. ___

**3** Lay's is the brand name used by the company all over the world. ___

**4** The speaker highlights the importance of visual symbols in marketing. ___

**5** The speaker attends a well-known tertiary education establishment. ___

**6** The 'Choose a flavour' campaigns are always global. ___

**7** The campaigns have positive results for both the company and the customer. ___

**8** During the campaign, Lay's make tens of thousands of new flavours. ___

**3** **Listen again and complete the notes in the table.**

| History | Campaign |
| --- | --- |
| Founded in 1932 by a(n) [1]_____ | General public asked to choose a new [6]_____ |
| Merged with Fritos in [2]_____ | Uses different [7]_____ to have conversations with customers |
| In 1965, merged with Pepsi Cola to create [3]_____ | Targets [8]_____ people |
| Still uses the original name Walkers in [4]_____ | Improves [9]_____ awareness and involves loyal customers |
| Incorporated the name Walkers into the global Lay's [5]_____ | Good marketing [10]_____ for the 21st century |

**Functional language**

## Changing the subject and staying on track

**1** **Choose the correct option in italics to complete the extract from a meeting.**

**A:** OK. Can we [1] *come / move* to item two on the agenda, updating our website?

**B:** Is this a [2] *well / good* moment to start talking about the prices for next year?

**A:** We'll get to the prices in a [3] *moment / time*. Can we first discuss the website and how we need to change it to get more international business? Sally? Can you give us your initial ideas?

**C:** OK. Well the main reason for the new look is to make it a more interactive website.

**B:** That [4] *reminds / remembers* me. I spent a couple of hours on some of our competitors' websites yesterday. They are very good.

**C:** I know. It's good to look at the competition. There will be [5] *much / plenty* of time for that later. However, first we need to look at ours. I think we need to make serious changes to it. It's slow, has very little video and is in only one language.

**A:** What languages do you think we need, Sally?

**C:** I'll [6] *go / come* to that later. Let's look at what we want from our website.

**A:** Before I [7] *forget / move*, marketing are joining us at 12.30 so we've got thirty minutes to finalise our ideas.

**B:** By the way … is there a chance to discuss functionality at some stage?

**C:** There is, but I really think we [8] *should / might* get to that when we know what we want from the site.

**B:** OK, no problem. But we need to discuss it at some point.

**C:** We will and I'm aware that it's a problem. OK … where was I?

## Reaching agreement

**2** **Complete the extract from a meeting using the words and phrases in the box.**

> afraid I disagree   don't agree with   Good idea   How about if   not a bad idea
> not sure I agree   right   should   Why don't we

**C:** So, these are some of my initial thoughts. We definitely need to invest in a smart, new website.

**B:** I'm [1]_____ with you on that. I think we should improve our current one.

**A:** I'm [2]_____ . Making changes would be a long and expensive business. We want something completely up-to-date with the best technology, don't you agree, Sally?

**C:** Yes, I think you're [3]_____ . With a new website, it should be easy to make our own changes in future. That will save us a lot of money.

**A:** Who is going to do it? I think we [4] _____ use the people we used last time.

**C:** Sorry, I [5]_____ you. I think they are expensive and old-fashioned. I have found a couple of young graduates who have done some brilliant work.

**A:** I'm not sure. That could be risky. [6]_____ ask three companies to make proposals?

**B:** [7]_____ ! Let's ask those two graduates and another company. Maybe one with international experience?

**C:** Actually, that's [8]_____ . What is our budget?

**B:** [9]_____ we write the specification and then see what offers we get?

**C:** I agree. Shall I work on that with Laura?

**A:** That's a good idea. Can you send me a draft next week?

**C:** No problem.

## Writing    Letter confirming an order

**1** Look at the paragraph guide below. Put the sentences a–g in the correct position in the letter on the right.

**a** You will be pleased to know that this has been included in the final price of $1,275 per month.

**b** We thank you for your business and look forward to working with you. If you have any queries, please do not hesitate to contact us.

**c** We discussed a discount of 15 percent providing you pay for the goods within one calendar month.

**d** We are writing to you to confirm your order number Y45364 for 200 sacks per month for 12 months, which we received by email yesterday.

**e** Payment terms are $1,275 monthly, 30 days after the date of the invoice and we enclose full terms and conditions for your records.

**f** As agreed on the telephone when we first talked about your order a few days ago, I confirm that we will deliver the sacks to your Brno outlet on the 28th of the month at a price of $7.50 per unit.

**g** We also confirm that the first delivery will be on 28th February.

| PARAGRAPH GUIDE | Dear Mr Stoff, |
|---|---|
| Paragraph 1:<br>confirm order<br>(sacks per month / duration) | 1 ___ |
| Paragraph 2:<br>refer to phone agreement | 2 ___ , 3 ___ , 4 ___ , 5 ___ |
| Paragraph 3:<br>payment terms, full T&Cs in separate document | 6 ___ |
| Paragraph 4:<br>thanks | 7 ___ |
|  | Yours sincerely,<br>Alain Chamel |

**2** Write a letter of about 150 words confirming an order from another company.

| | | |
|---|---|---|
| **Item:** | Desk Lamps – Model PWB2 | |
| **Order number:** | IX765 | *OK* |
| **Quantity:** | 80 | |
| **Unit price:** | $40 (including discount) | |
| **Discount:** | 20% on orders over 80 units | *agreed last week* |
| **Terms:** | 30 days | *after date on invoice. New customer!* |
| **Delivery date:** | 5th May | *send business terms and conditions with invoice (and new catalogue!)* |
| **Delivery to:** | BRF, 12, Tristram Street, Perth | |

- Begin and end appropriately.

- Open by giving order and delivery details.

- Clarify payment terms.

- Refer to any other documents which you have enclosed.

## Vocabulary    Technological innovation

**1** Correct the underlined words in the text.

Many businesses are successful because they [1] ~~swipe~~ disrupt established industries with new ideas which change everything in an almost [2] customise way. After these changes, we never go back. In the 1950s, the transistor radio arrived and suddenly families had a(an) [3] place about which music to listen to. This changed the music industry completely as young people had more influence and did not have to listen to their parents' music. Another disruption came with MP3 players in the 2000s, when people could [4] interacting their music libraries by buying any track they wanted. By [5] automated with other people on the internet, they could even share their playlists as well. Certain entrepreneurs saw an opportunity and soon everyone could [6] disrupt an order for any music (or indeed any item) and receive it almost immediately with just a(an) [7] choice of a credit card. Such purchasing trends are beneficial to companies such as Amazon and Apple who save money on orders with no delivery cost and reduce their costs on delivered goods by introducing other [8] magical processes in their warehouses; these include changes to machinery that reduce the need for human labour – an increasingly typical result of technological innovation.

## Describing innovative products

**2** Choose the correct option in italics.

**A:** Have you seen my new smartphone?

**B:** Wow! That's very [1] *stylish / advanced*. You're always so fashionable. Was it expensive?

**A:** It's [2] *top of the range / user friendly* so it wasn't cheap.

**B:** Why did you change?

**A:** Well, my last smartphone wasn't [3] *innovative / dependable*. It was always crashing. Have you still got the same one?

**B:** Yeah, same old phone. It's [4] *unique / classic*. Nothing special at all but I like it.

**A:** Your watch is pretty cool though! I've never seen one like that before. Is it [5] *advanced / unique*?

**B:** No, it's not. I got it in the USA last month, they're quite popular there. It's very [6] *well designed / classic* though. Really light to wear and the functions are really easy to use.

**3** Complete the words in the text.

**1** With its cl _ _ _ _ c design from the 1960s updated for the 21st century, this car looks beautiful. Each one is un _ _ _ e, as it is customised to suit your personal tastes.

**2** Made from titanium, this pen is incredibly tough and can write underwater and in zero gravity! It is the perfect combination of st _ _ _ _ h design and in _ _ _ _ _ _ _ ve technology.

**3** This t _ _ -of-t _ _ -r _ _ ge TV is ultra-slim and expensive as a result. But it is w _ _ _ d _ _ _ _ _ ed and will look perfect in any living room. With its a _ _ _ _ _ _ ed technology the picture is absolutely perfect.

**4** This tablet has the bonus of its own projector, which is easy to set up and give presentations, so it is extremely u _ _ _ -f _ _ _ _ _ _ ly. With a long battery life, it is also d _ _ _ _ _ _ _ le. Great for the business traveller!

## Grammar  Present Perfect Simple with *just, already* and *yet*

**1** **Put the words in the correct order to complete the sentences.**

**1** a / smartphone / I / ordered / new / just / have

_____

**2** candidates / already / we / interviewed / have / three

_____

**3** yet / you / have / lunch / had / ?

_____

**4** ticket / I / already / have / booked / my

_____

**5** a / yet / found / have / you / solution / ?

_____

**6** yet / started / two / I / but / finished / hours / haven't / ago / I

_____

**7** point / am / we / afraid / have / already / I / that / discussed

_____

**8** left / I / but / she / just / sorry / am / has

_____

**2** **Match the questions (1–8) with the responses (a–h).**

**1** Do you want to come for lunch?

**2** Could I speak to Maria, please?

**3** Could I take a look at your report?

**4** Have you booked the flights?

**5** Have you seen Juan and Mario today?

**6** Could you tell me where the meeting is?

**7** Can I have your number?

**8** Have you heard from Carla?

**a** Room 121 but they've already started.

**b** No, not yet. I'll do it now.

**c** Yes, she's just called.

**d** Thanks, but I've already eaten.

**e** I'm afraid she's just left.

**f** I think I've already given it to you. It's on my card.

**g** Sorry but I haven't finished it yet.

**h** Yes, I've just seen them in the cafeteria.

**3** **Complete the sentences and questions using the words in the box.**

already   just   yet (x2)

**1**

**A:** Have you paid that invoice _____ ?

**B:** Yes, I've _____ paid it. I'm printing off the confirmation now.

**2**

**A:** Can you do that translation for me?

**B:** I've _____ done it! I emailed it to you last night.

**3**

**A:** Do you want me to check the contract?

**B:** We haven't got it _____. They only posted it yesterday.

**Listening**

**1** 🔊 5.01 **Listen to the radio programme and choose the correct option.**

**1** What does Steven do?

   **a** He works for an airline company.

   **b** He works as a test driver.

   **c** He's retired.

**2** He got the job when

   **a** he left school.

   **b** he visited the circuit.

   **c** the previous test driver stopped work.

**3** How often does Steven have accidents?

   **a** never

   **b** hardly ever

   **c** quite often

**4** After the tests

   **a** he is allowed to keep the car.

   **b** he drives home in a luxury car.

   **c** he drives home in his own car.

**5** Who does Penny work for?

   **a** her own company

   **b** her husband

   **c** a group of restaurants

**6** Her job involves

   **a** serving in restaurants.

   **b** cooking the dishes.

   **c** helping create new dishes.

**7** What does she often have to do?

   **a** find new chefs

   **b** test the same dish

   **c** inform her boss of problems

**8** The mystery shoppers

   **a** come from the general public.

   **b** work for the chain.

   **c** know all the chefs.

**2** **Listen again and complete the table.**

| Steven ... | Penny ... |
|---|---|
| tests [1]_____ cars. | works in quality [5]_____ . |
| checks the cars work well and [2]_____ . | checks the food is up to [6]_____ . |
| makes sure they are comfortable, fast and [3]_____ . | reports problems and tries to find [7]_____ . |
| has to test them in [4]_____ weather. | uses mystery shoppers who write a report in return for a free [8]_____ . |

**Functional language**

## Asking open and closed questions

**1** Complete the questions using a suitable verb.

1
> **A:** What do you _____ , a problem with dates?

> **B:** Well, the schedule needs revising.

2
> **A:** Can you _____ back to us by next Monday?

> **B:** That will be fine. By email?

3
> **A:** _____ it possible to change the date of the presentation?

> **B:** We should be able to. I'll speak to the Sales Manager.

4
> **A:** Why _____ they want to extend the deadline for delivery?

> **B:** Because they don't have enough staff at the moment.

5
> **A:** How long will it _____ you to get the new parts?

> **B:** I think about a week if we're lucky.

6
> **A:** Jo, what do you _____ ?

> **B:** I quite like the idea. It's simple to do.

7
> **A:** _____ us about the meeting with the client.

> **B:** I think it went really well …

8
> **A:** What _____ wrong with the new version?

> **B:** It needs better sound and clearer graphics.

## Describing features and benefits

**2** Read the discussion about a corporate gift. Choose the correct option in italics.

**A:** This looks interesting, Yumi. But what is it exactly?

**B:** It's a powerbank. It's a portable charger for a smartphone.

**A:** It would be quite big to carry around. Do you think it would fit into a suit pocket?

**B:** It probably would. It [1] *measures / makes* 11 cm by 5 cm. And it's about 2 cm thick. That's small for a charger.

**A:** I suppose so. Is it heavy?

**B:** It [2] *heavy / weighs* about 450 g.

**A:** So, how long does it take to charge a smartphone?

**B:** 30 minutes.

**A:** And how many times can it charge it?

**B:** Six complete charges. And it comes with two outputs.

**A:** So, what does that mean?

**B:** That [3] *means / lets* that you can charge two smartphones at the same time.

**A:** That's good. What colours can we choose from?

**B:** It comes [4] *in / with* blue or black.

**A:** Is that the case? What's it made [5] *from / of?*

**B:** Hard plastic. It just [6] *means / makes* that it's easier to protect it. It comes [7] *in / with* cables as well, so it allows you to have everything you need in one place.

**A:** I think it's a great idea. It [8] *lets / means* you charge your phone anytime, anywhere. Brilliant for long journeys. What about price?

**B:** Within the budget you gave me.

**A:** Good work, Yumi.

## Writing Product review

**1A Read the product review and correct the mistakes.**

I [1]~~choose~~ this Bluetooth speaker because the reviews were positive and the information on the website [2]told it performed as well as more expensive ones. So, I [3]decision to buy it because it was pretty good value for money. [4]That I like most is that the sound quality is great. I was [5]impression by the coloured lights which flash as the music plays. I [6]particular like the fact that it is very light and quite small so it is good for travelling.

However, there are some problems. The main [7]upside is that I spent hours trying to connect it to my phone. [8]Other problem is that the charge doesn't last long so I can't use it very long outside. Also, the instructions were not included, which was annoying. One last [9]think I don't like is the case. It is very poor quality.

Unfortunately, I can only give it two stars.

★★☆☆☆  >

| | | |
|---|---|---|
| 1 _chose_ | 4 _____ | 7 _____ |
| 2 _____ | 5 _____ | 8 _____ |
| 3 _____ | 6 _____ | 9 _____ |

**B How did the writer organise the product review in Exercise 1A? Complete the table using the aspects in the box.**

battery life   case   size   good price   instructions   lights   good reviews
sound quality   technical issues   two-star rating

| Reasons for buying | Good points | Bad points | Conclusion |
|---|---|---|---|
|  |  |  |  |

**2 Write a product review of about 150 words using the notes below. Include the following:**

- a clear introduction.
- good points about the product.
- bad points about the product.
- a clear conclusion.

- *wanted a tablet to watch films when travelling*
- *bought it because a colleague had one*
- *read a lot of reviews first*
- *got a very good price – 25 percent cheaper than other brands*
- *good size screen*
- *easy to use*

- *clear graphics*
- *volume is not very loud – hard to hear even with headphones*
- *battery is very poor – only lasts three hours*
- *screen always dirty*
- *next time, buy a more expensive one*
- *three stars only*

**Vocabulary** **Health and safety**

**1** Choose the correct option in italics.

**A:** Do you have to wear special clothing for work?

**B:** Yes. Everyone is [1]*handled / issued* with personal safety equipment and clothing.

**A:** What do you have for your hands?

**B:** We wear cut-resistant gloves because we have to [2]*fit / handle* sharp debris sometimes.

**A:** Does the job [3]*pose / record* a risk of injury?

**B:** Yes, a small risk, but it's not terribly dangerous. And they [4]*pose / hold* regular training programmes about safety. All the boats are also [5]*fitted / held* with cameras so we can see what happened if there's an accident. What about you? Are there lots of health and safety rules where you work?

**A:** Not really, but then my job isn't dangerous like yours. But we still have to [6]*issue / record* all accidents in a book.

**2** Complete the text using the words and phrases in the box.

> cut-resistant gloves   ear defenders   face mask   goggles   hard hat
> high-visibility clothing   steel toe-cap boots

## What do **I WEAR** to work?   The construction worker

We have to wear [1]_____ because we work a lot in the dark and we have
[2]_____ to protect our feet. On a cold day, it is good to have the [3]_____
because they keep our ears warm and they also help with the noise, of course! For our hands, we
have [4]_____ and we sometimes wear a(n) [5]_____ to protect our faces.
We have to wear a(n) [6]_____ at all times outside to protect our heads. Mine is bright
yellow and has my name on so I can be identified! The last thing I wear is [7]_____ to
protect my eyes on certain jobs.

**3** Complete the text with suitable words.

**A bad day at the office**

It was Friday 13th at our office last week and we had a terrible day. Nearly everyone on the staff [1]h __ __ __
themselves. It was winter and our receptionist [2]s __ __ __ p __ __ on some ice on her way to work. She
[3]f __ __ __ on the pavement and landed on some glass. As a result, she [4]c __ __ her hand badly; there
was so much blood she had to go to hospital. Another colleague arrived safely at work but [5]d __ __ __ p __ __
a box of paper on his foot and [6]b __ __ k __ a toe. So, he went to hospital as well. Another colleague
walked into a door and [7]h __ __ his head. He hit it so hard that he actually [8]d __ m __ __ __ d the door!
His nose started to [9]b __ __ __ d a lot so I drove him to the hospital as well. At that point, I decided to close
the office for the rest of the day before I [10]i __ j __ __ __ d myself!

## Grammar   Modal verbs of prohibition, obligation and no obligation

**1** Match the questions (1–8) with the responses (a–h).

1 Did you work long hours?
2 What was the dress code?
3 Can I make personal calls?
4 Can we use the internet?
5 What language do we use?
6 What happened if you were late?
7 What do I do with my badge?
8 What happened if you were ill?

a You mustn't make them during working hours.
b You have to wear it at all times.
c All documents have to be in English.
d You had to have a doctor's note after two days.
e I didn't have to call. My boss was fine about it.
f You mustn't use it, except at lunchtime.
g Yes! At least once a week I needed to work late just to finish.
h You didn't need to wear a suit but you had to be smart.

**2** Choose the correct option in italics.

Hello everybody and welcome to the company! I'll just spend a minute or two on some rules and regulations. First of all, your ID badge. You ¹ *must / don't need to* have it with you at all times for security reasons. If you forget it one day, you can get a temporary one at reception but you ² *have to / mustn't* keep it for more than 24 hours. We issue you all with mobile phones but you ³ *don't need to / mustn't* use them for personal calls. If you ⁴ *don't have to / have to* make a personal call at work, you ⁵ *must / don't need to* go into a meeting room and use your own phone. As you know, our dress code is quite relaxed – men ⁶ *don't have to / must* wear a tie although everyone ⁷ *doesn't need to / needs to* look smart and professional. Everyone ⁸ *has to / doesn't need to* be at work between 10 and 4, and you ⁹ *must / don't have to* do at least two more hours outside these times. Don't forget that as well as your paid holiday, you can all take an extra three days off in the year and you ¹⁰ *don't need to / must* explain why. I think that's all for now. Any questions?

**3** Complete the sentences using the phrases in the box.

| didn't need to   don't have to   had to   has to   have to   mustn't |
| --- |

1 You _____ work weekends here but they pay you double so I sometimes do when I need the extra money.

2 In my last job I _____ wear special clothing but I do now.

3 Her contract says she _____ work for a similar company if she leaves.

4 If he leaves, he _____ give three months' notice.

5 In my current job I _____ work 40 hours per week, which is a lot! I'm never home before 7 p.m.

6 Where my wife worked before, she _____ work on Saturdays. She hated it!

## Reading

# Looking for job security?

# Get a job in security

Security is one of the fastest growing industries in the world. Thirty years ago, we didn't have to wait in line for half an hour at a sports event or a museum to show the contents of our bag. We didn't need to have so many guards watching people in shops to make sure they didn't steal anything. Now stores have both guards and automatic systems to scan you as you enter and leave. All of this security requires not only top-class equipment but also lots of workers. Security is big business.

In developing countries, private security guards are often employed in larger numbers than official police officers. Wealthy people are afraid of crime against their property or their families, such as robbery or kidnapping. A large number of security guards are employed and state-of-the-art surveillance equipment is fitted in most luxury houses. Computer experts are needed to design all that equipment.

In many countries, there are now certain areas or towns that organise their own security when they are unhappy with the security the state can offer. In most countries, the number of

police officers and prison guards that the local authorities can afford to provide is declining; this opens opportunities for security firms to manage prisons or transport criminals. Around the world governments are very happy to pay a private company to do this.

Large corporations pay millions of dollars these days to keep their information technology systems safe from hackers and competitors. They also need to keep an eye on their own employees and have special staff to monitor email and report back on any unusual activity.

The financial world has also become an important area for security experts, too. These days banks have to defend themselves against all sorts of white collar crimes such as fraud or money laundering. All in all, an industry which in the past was reserved for retired boxers is now one of the largest industries in the world, employing millions of people and offering a vast range of opportunities to all involved.

**1** Read the article and put the topics in the order they are mentioned.

**A** Solutions for the rich ___    **D** Changes over the last decades ___

**B** Money crimes ___    **E** Taking over from traditional security forces ___

**C** The corporate world ___

**2** Read the article again and complete the sentences using the words and phrases in the box. Some are <u>not</u> used.

| companies    careers    hackers    workers    police    prisons    technology |
| the right equipment    their employees    their families |

**1** The security business needs lots of _____ .

**2** Rich people are worried about _____ .

**3** In many countries there aren't enough _____ .

**4** _____ are a danger to corporate information technology systems.

**5** Companies use security systems to monitor _____ .

**6** Security is a business which offers good _____ .

**3** Complete the notes in the table.

| Retail | Rich people | Countries | Corporations and banks |
|---|---|---|---|
| Guards watch customers to check they don't 1_____ . | They are afraid of crimes such as 3_____ or kidnapping. | In certain countries, there are less and less police officers and more and more 5_____ security guards. | Special staff are used to 7_____ email in certain companies. |
| Shops monitor customers as they enter and 2_____ . | They employ private security guards and pay for security companies to install the very latest security 4_____ . | Private companies now manage 6_____ in lots of countries. | They need to defend themselves against 8_____ and money laundering. |

**Functional language**

### Explaining rules and requirements

**1** Complete the conversation using the phrases in the box. There is one extra phrase.

| | | |
|---|---|---|
| don't need to worry about | I understand that | it's a question of |
| it's great that you | has to be | my position is | needs signing |
| we can't agree unless | we really appreciate all | |

**A:** So, tell me Josh, what's on your mind?

**B:** Some friends are planning to do a charity bike ride in the USA and the thing is, I'd like to go with them. The ride is three weeks, but I'd like to take six weeks holiday.

**A:** Six weeks is a long time and you've only been working here for nine months.
¹_____ want to do it, but you don't have enough holiday.

**B:** ²_____ this could be a problem but I'm happy to take time off unpaid.

**A:** I'm sorry but ³_____ policy. No unpaid holiday is normally permitted in your first year.

**B:** But I haven't had a single day off in nine months!

**A:** I know you haven't and ⁴_____ your work but you're only allowed to take four weeks in a complete first year. ⁵_____ clear.

**B:** Well, could I take four weeks now and no more for the rest of the year?

**A:** I know this is difficult but ⁶_____ there are special circumstances. How about three weeks?

**B:** OK, that can work! What do I need to do next?

**A:** A holiday form ⁷_____ by your manager. It ⁸_____ signed two weeks in advance, but I would ask her to do it now. Tell her you've discussed it with me!

### Resolving a conflict

**2** Put the dialogue in the correct order (1–11). Two lines have been done for you.

**a** I can see how annoying it is for everyone, but he is our best salesman and hits his targets. Why don't you try discussing it with him? ___

**b** My suggestion is to give him more responsibility and more work. And limit personal internet time for everyone. Do you agree? ___

**c** There's another problem with Andrea. He uses the internet all day but not for work. _1_

**d** Yes, I think he needs that. Can I just check senior management are happy with that plan? ___

**e** I know it's not, but he can't do whatever he wants. I think we need to come to a compromise over this – the team aren't happy about it because they are so busy. ___

**f** OK, I'll try it for a month. I'll also speak to Andrea this week, privately. I'll tell him I want to give him more responsibility. ___

**g** I totally agree. I'd like to make the internet limit an official policy. How do we proceed? ___

**h** I'll discuss it with him, but if I can't stop him using the internet, what do you suggest? ___

**i** It might be a good idea to think about the exact details first. Then explain the policy in a team meeting, and review the situation next month. ___

**j** Of course. Let me know as soon as you hear from them. _11_

**k** I know how you feel about this, but it is not against the rules to use the internet at work. ___

## Writing   Instructions and warnings

**1** Read the general instructions from a company handbook. Decide if they are Dos, Don'ts or Warnings.

### A few things to remember

- No one is permitted to use technical equipment without training.
- Report any faulty equipment to your manager.
- You are not allowed to eat while working.
- Watch out for wet floors.

- Follow safety instructions carefully.
- Don't remove company property.
- You must wear your name badge at all times.
- Be careful not to damage company equipment.

**2** Read this email from the Human Resources Manager (Carla), requesting some health and safety guidelines. Imagine you are Matteo and write the guidelines, giving staff information on health and safety. Write about 120 words.

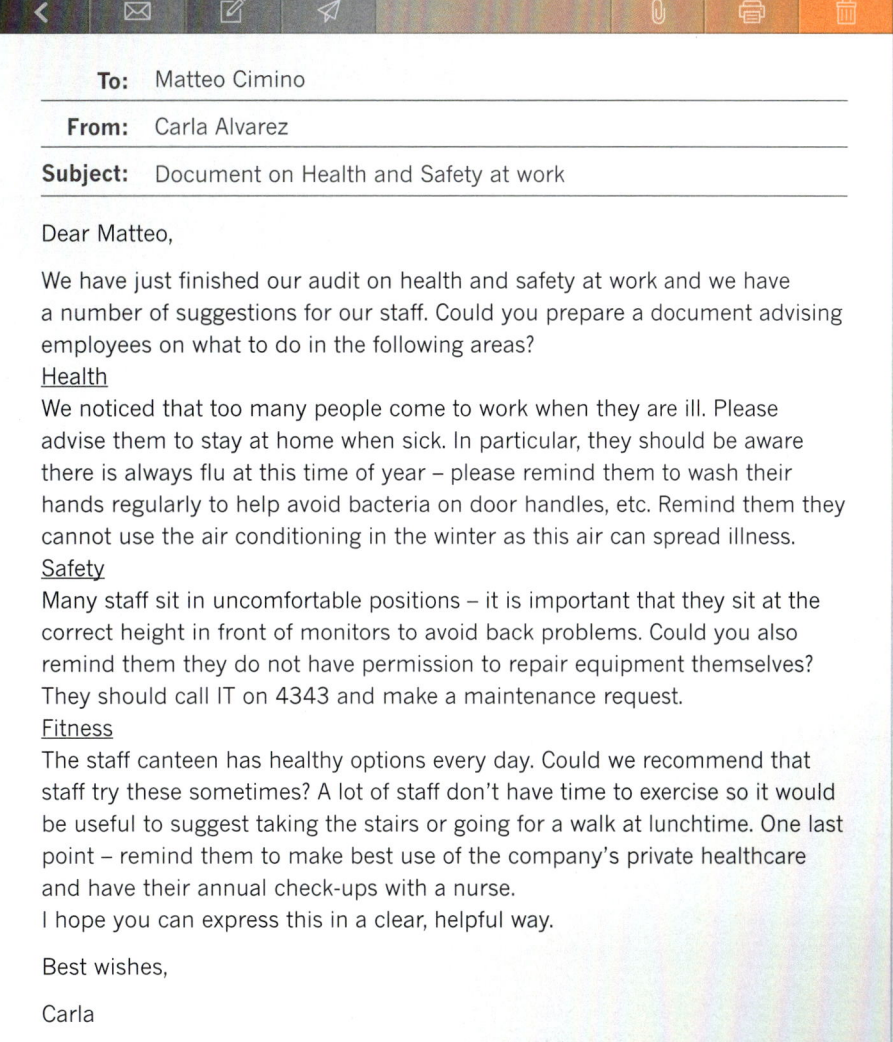

**To:** Matteo Cimino

**From:** Carla Alvarez

**Subject:** Document on Health and Safety at work

Dear Matteo,

We have just finished our audit on health and safety at work and we have a number of suggestions for our staff. Could you prepare a document advising employees on what to do in the following areas?

Health

We noticed that too many people come to work when they are ill. Please advise them to stay at home when sick. In particular, they should be aware there is always flu at this time of year – please remind them to wash their hands regularly to help avoid bacteria on door handles, etc. Remind them they cannot use the air conditioning in the winter as this air can spread illness.

Safety

Many staff sit in uncomfortable positions – it is important that they sit at the correct height in front of monitors to avoid back problems. Could you also remind them they do not have permission to repair equipment themselves? They should call IT on 4343 and make a maintenance request.

Fitness

The staff canteen has healthy options every day. Could we recommend that staff try these sometimes? A lot of staff don't have time to exercise so it would be useful to suggest taking the stairs or going for a walk at lunchtime. One last point – remind them to make best use of the company's private healthcare and have their annual check-ups with a nurse.

I hope you can express this in a clear, helpful way.

Best wishes,

Carla

- Organise your instructions and warnings into sections for 'Health', 'Safety' and 'Fitness'.

- Include all the points in the notes.

- Use some of the following phrases to avoid sounding repetitive: *beware of, don't, no one is permitted to, make sure, must, you're not allowed to, don't forget to, watch out for.*

## Vocabulary    Customer service

### 1 Complete the conversation using suitable words.

**A:** Good to see you again, Giorgio. When did you arrive?

**G:** Very late last night, Amelia, after a terrible flight. We left late, there was no food and absolutely no priority ¹ b _ _ _ d _ _ _ _  even though we had paid an extra £30 to get on first!

**A:** Really? Who did you fly with?

**G:** One of those budget airlines. It was definitely a(n) ² N _-f _ _ _ _ l _  flight!

**A:** Oh, unlucky. I got an upgrade to business ³ _ _ a _ _ _ ! It was a real ⁴ p _ _ m _ _ _ m service. There was great personal ⁵ a _ t _ _ _ _ _ n. There were twelve passengers and three cabin crew!

**G:** Sounds amazing!

**A:** It was! We got such VIP ⁶ tr _ _ t _ _ _ _ t, hot towels, cold drinks, beautiful food …

**G:** Very different from my experience! Next time I should fly with you!

### 2 Choose the correct option in italics.

**Subject:** Complaint about recent flight

Dear Sir or Madam,

I am a regular passenger with your airline and I am usually very ¹ *satisfying / satisfied*. Unfortunately, on a recent flight to Athens your staff were not very ² *helpful / helpless*. Firstly, the woman sitting next to me was very ³ *anxiety / anxious* and I called for ⁴ *assist / assistance* but nobody came. I know passengers can be very ⁵ *undemanding / demanding* but worried passengers need to be looked after.
Then, the person sitting on my left ⁶ *requested / request* a glass of water. It took fifteen minutes before he got the water but nobody ⁷ *apologetic / apologised*. Generally, on this flight the crew lacked ⁸ *empathy / empathetic* and ⁹ *handling / handled* a number of situations badly.
I hope I can feel ¹⁰ *confident / confidence* the next time I fly with you.

Yours faithfully,

Emma Hobbs

### 3 Put the words in the correct order to complete the sentences.

1 was / take-off / the / probably / anxious / about / passenger

_____

2 about / aren't / a / people / confident / lot / flying / of

_____

3 nobody / passengers / to / offered / the / unfortunately / anxious / assistance

_____

4 for / the / passengers / flight attendant / apologise / to / the / the / delay / didn't

_____

5 service / passengers / was / the / neither / satisfied / with / of / the

_____

## Grammar Verbs + *to*-infinitive or *-ing*

**1 Match the questions (1–6) with the responses (a–f).**

1 Did you mention it to your manager?

2 Have you met the new Sales Director?

3 Who have they decided to work with?

4 Have they found someone for the project?

5 Did you remember to call the hotel?

6 Have you found your passport yet?

a No, but I remember putting it in my bag.

b Yes, Alfredo has agreed to manage it.

c No, I saw him but I forgot to tell him.

d Yes, I called them last night.

e I think they chose a German company.

f No, I wanted to say hello but she was busy.

**2 Choose the correct option in italics.**

**A:** Who's that over there?

**B:** That's the Customer Care Director. Do you remember ¹ *to meet / meeting* him last year at the sales conference?

**A:** Yes, of course. He's here to talk about his department. Did you hear about our main competitor?

**B:** No. What happened?

**A:** They've lost a lot of business. And unless they improve their systems, they risk ² *to lose / losing* more customers.

**B:** Really?

**A:** Yes. Apparently, their largest customer is considering ³ *to changing / change* suppliers.

**B:** What happened?

**A:** They failed ⁴ *to realise / realising* the importance of good customer service! There were some problems and the customer asked for a discount.

**B:** With unhappy customers, I always agree ⁵ *to reduce / reducing* the price the next time.

**A:** Me, too. Do you want ⁶ *to meet up / meeting up* for dinner later? I'll pay!

**3 Complete the text using the correct form of the words in the box.**

| book call stay use waste write |
| --- |

I wanted ¹ _____ a holiday in Italy and a friend recommended ² _____ a website called roomz.com. I registered, but unfortunately I didn't remember ³ _____ down my password. Anyway, I booked my room and then went out shopping. When I came back an hour later, I hadn't received the confirmation email, so I tried to log in but I couldn't remember the password. So, I decided ⁴ _____ Customer Services but they couldn't find my booking. I couldn't afford ⁵ _____ any more time so at this point I called the hotel directly. They were very polite but obviously couldn't find my booking either. I told the person I spoke to that I would still like ⁶ _____ in their hotel and she made the booking for me.

## Reading

# The customer is not always king

*Julia, 25.* We flew to Florianopolis for a relaxing, short break before my wedding. There were eight of us. We booked a villa with a pool and the plan was to be there for a week. We had a brilliant five days, but on the Friday, completely out of the blue, we got an email from our airline telling us our flight back to Sao Paolo on Sunday was cancelled. No other information. We were told we could book another flight but the next one was on the Wednesday! We tried to telephone our airline but they didn't answer. Their website crashed the next day because they had cancelled so many flights. They said we would get our money back but no news so far. We tried other airlines and managed to get three tickets for the Sunday but the rest of us had to book a coach back. Our journey back was awful – it took fifteen hours because the coach broke down, not the two hours we were expecting at the start of the week. I promise I will never fly with that airline again. Definitely 'no frills'!

*Roberto, 35.* We needed to book a car for our holiday in Florida last September. I made the booking online but unfortunately I had booked it to start the next day, not the following Monday. Later that day I checked the confirmation email and realised my mistake. I went online and entered the booking number but I was told that it was too late to change. It was annoying because it was my own mistake. Anyway, at the top of the screen was a telephone number and I decided to call it. They answered the phone immediately and asked what the problem was. I said it was completely my fault and probably too late to change the booking. The young man replied that there was no problem and in fact it would be $50 cheaper! He changed the booking and repaid the difference within five minutes. Brilliant service. It was my fault after all.

**1** Read the article and decide if Julia and Roberto would describe their customer service experience as positive (✔) or negative (✗).

Julia ☐ Roberto ☐

**2** Read the article again and decide if these statements are *true* (T) or *false* (F).

**1** Julia booked a holiday for five days. ___

**2** Her group bought alternative flights for the return date. ___

**3** Luckily, there were no problems with the bus journey. ___

**4** Roberto couldn't change his booking online. ___

**5** He had to wait a long time when he phoned. ___

**6** He knew he had made the mistake. ___

**3** Choose the correct option.

**1** Why did Julia go away with her friends?

   **a** to see Sao Paolo

   **b** to relax before her wedding

   **c** to attend a friend's wedding

**2** They got new flights

   **a** for the following week.

   **b** for three of the group.

   **c** within fifteen hours.

**3** What mistake did Roberto make when booking his car?

   **a** He booked it from the wrong place.

   **b** He booked it with the wrong company.

   **c** He booked it from the wrong date.

**4** The new dates for his booking

   **a** were the following month.

   **b** were less expensive.

   **c** were booked online.

## Functional language

### Responding to customer concerns

**1** Complete the conversation using the phrases in the box.

> correct about that   has filled me in on the   has told me about that
> I'll go through   I'm sure   let me   please, understand that I see
> we'll come up with a   your side of things

**A:** Good evening, Madam. I hear that you're not happy with your room. My colleague, Claudia, [1]_____ details. Could you tell me again? I just want to hear [2]_____ .

**B:** Basically, I stay here quite often and I always get a room with a bath, not a shower. I also like the 4th floor.

**A:** Yes. Claudia [3]_____ .

**B:** I explained to your colleague but she said you were full and I couldn't change. She said I should speak to you.

**A:** Claudia is [4]_____ . We are full and because you were the last to check in, she couldn't make a change.

**B:** So, will you be able to do anything about it?

**A:** [5]_____ the bookings and see if we can make a late change. Why don't you have dinner and come back and see me in an hour or so?

**B:** Sorry, but I'm not at all hungry. I just want a bath. I'm a regular customer here, and that's the only thing I ask for.

**A:** [6]_____ your point, but I'm afraid you'll have to wait. Why don't you wait in the bar?

**B:** OK. But do you think you will find a solution?

**A:** Yes, I'm confident [7]_____ solution. I just need an hour or so. [8]_____ speak to my colleagues. [9]_____ we'll find you a room with a bath. Hopefully on the 4th floor!

**B:** Thank you so much. I'll come back in an hour.

### Discussing and presenting ideas

**2** Read the suggestions between colleagues discussing improving their English. Put the words in the correct order to complete the sentences.

> The training is over for another year. How are we going to keep improving our English?

1 _____
(do / need / the / thing / we / first / to) is to have an English homepage on our computers.

3 _____
(of / idea / like / team / would / to / push / the / our) having lunch in English at least twice a week.

2 _____
(the / of / idea / came / our / up / team / with) listening to the news every day in English. Just ten minutes of listening is useful.

4 _____
(suggest / everyone / to / needs / we) read a short story every week and discuss it.

> They are all good ideas. 5 _____
> (is / be / thing / to / it's / got / the) easy.

## Writing   External 'thank you' email

**1A**   Put the sentences (a–g) of the 'thank you' email in the correct order.

Dear Henri,

___ (a) Kind regards,

___ (b) I would also like to express our appreciation for the way you handled the last minute changes we made when we realised we would need two extra analysts and that both of them would need to speak Portuguese.

___ (c) Thank you and your staff once again for all your hard work. I look forward to working with you on other projects.

_1_ (d) I am writing to thank you and your team for your excellent recruitment services. Thanks to your hard work we now have six excellent new employees.

___ (e) Pietro sorted out that problem very quickly and found us two excellent people.

___ (f) Can I conclude by saying you showed great professionalism, patience and good humour throughout the project.

___ (g) We will definitely use your company again in the future and have already recommended you to other companies in the industry.

Frauke Hein

**B**   How did the writer organise the email in Exercise 1A? Complete the table with the letters a–g.

| Beginning | Details | Closing |
|---|---|---|
|  |  |  |

**2**   Use the notes below to write a 'thank you' email of about 140 words to a supplier.

– design company run by Diana
– designed a 10th anniversary brochure
– design was beautiful
– their team was creative and hard-working
– they agreed to include some extra photos we sent very late
– the price was good value
– the designer (Velleda) was really patient
– the company hope to work with them again
– we have given their name to your professional association

- Write three parts – beginning, details and closing.
- Mention a particular problem.
- Mention a specific person who did very well.

# 8 > Communication

## Vocabulary   Digital communication

**1** Choose the correct option in italics.

---

### ✉ Checklist for dealing with emails at work

☐ Try not to [1] *receive / check* your email too often.

☐ [2] *Catch up on / Delete* all your emails once or twice a day.

☐ When you have lots of emails, prioritise. [3] *Reply / Manage* to the most urgent first.

☐ When you send a(n) [4] *internal / social* email, always use professional language.

☐ Be the [5] *master / servant* of your inbox! Keep control by deleting unimportant emails so that you don't [6] *manage / overload* it.

---

**2** Complete the conversation using suitable words from Exercise 1.

**S:** How's the project coming along, Tomas?

**T:** Not too bad, thanks, Sophie, but I'm so busy. The problem is that people [1]_____ me with messages and emails.

**S:** Is that because of the project?

**T:** Not really. A lot of them are [2]_____ emails where colleagues have copied me in and they didn't have to. Very few of them are important.

**S:** When do you deal with them?

**T:** I always [3]_____ them first thing in the morning, and delete a lot. Later in the morning, I [4]_____ on them properly and [5]_____ to the important ones.

**S:** It sounds to me like you are organised, Tomas. You have [6]_____ the skill of dealing with emails anyway.

**T:** That's probably because I have to read so many!

**3** Complete the sentences using the words in the box.

> choice   concentrate   encourage
> engaged   improve   productive

**1** My company is keen to try anything which will _____ communication.

**2** When making a presentation, remember the audience will only stay _____ for a short time.

**3** It's good to provide a(n) _____ of dates when trying to set up a meeting.

**4** When I am talking to a colleague, I try to _____ on listening actively.

**5** I've had a very _____ morning and read all my urgent emails.

**6** We _____ all employees to delete unread emails on a weekly basis.

**Grammar**    **First and second conditional**

**1** **Complete the conversation using the missing phrases.**

**a** if the staff don't see the benefits

**b** if we all keep documents there

**c** it won't work

**d** if there are fewer walls

**e** people will communicate better

**A:** I hear your offices are being redesigned. How do you feel about it?

**B:** I'm not sure. The management think it will improve communication.

**A:** Really? What's their thinking?

**B:** If there are soft areas for chatting, [1] _____ .

**A:** Oh, I see. What about the open plan offices?

**B:** They think that [2] _____ , people will talk more.

**A:** And are there any other changes?

**B:** Yes. There is a new platform for sharing information internally. Everything will be much more efficient [3] _____ . I think it's a good idea. But [4] _____ if certain people refuse to use it.

**A:** And do you think that will happen?

**B:** Well … it's like all changes – [5] _____ , they won't use it. If they do, …

**2** **Match 1–6 with a–f to complete the sentences.**

**1** If we didn't have so many deadlines,

**2** Would the team understand more

**3** If we used social media more,

**4** You would make a lot of contacts

**5** If you sent it by email with a link,

**6** If the technology didn't exist,

**a** I think we'd get more business.

**b** everything would take much more time.

**c** they would get the information immediately.

**d** if the project leader explained things more clearly?

**e** if you went to some conferences.

**f** I wouldn't be so stressed.

**3** **Complete the sentences with the words in the box.**

| didn't   doesn't   don't   might   will   won't   wouldn't |
| --- |

**1** I _____ call a couple of customers if I have time this afternoon.

**2** If I were you, I _____ spend so much time catching up on emails.

**3** If she _____ spend so much time on the phone, she could finish earlier.

**4** If we don't finish this report on time, I _____ go to the meeting.

**5** I think we _____ be more efficient if we worked from home one day per week.

**6** He won't meet our Dutch customers if he _____ attend the webinar.

**7** If I _____ see you this afternoon, I'll definitely see you tomorrow.

**Listening**

**1** 🔊 8.01 **Listen to the podcast and put the topics in the order they are mentioned.**

**a** communication skills needed by a good manager ___

**b** choosing the right language to use ___

**c** coming to a conclusion through discussion ___

**d** deciding whether to email or phone ___

**e** being quiet if you don't know the answer ___

**2 Listen again and choose the correct option.**

**1** Andreas Hammer believes certain people

    **a** speak without thinking.

    **b** don't like meetings.

    **c** never know the answer.

**2** He thinks that in meetings people

    **a** talk too much.

    **b** need to share ideas more.

    **c** discuss ideas too much.

**3** According to Andreas the workplace

    **a** is like college.

    **b** is usually casual.

    **c** is more formal than university.

**4** What does Andreas say people need to learn to do?

    **a** write emails

    **b** make phone calls

    **c** choose the right way to communicate

**5** Managers

    **a** usually communicate well.

    **b** need to be better communicators than others.

    **c** are not always good communicators.

**6** Managers have to communicate to their team

    **a** in writing.

    **b** as a group.

    **c** on a personal basis.

**3 Complete the notes in the table.**

| Skills to develop | How to communicate | Good managers |
|---|---|---|
| Learn how to say $^1$_____ at first and think about the question. | Decide the best $^3$_____ of communicating: face to face, email, etc. | They have to communicate to the staff $^5$_____ made by the directors. |
| Learn how to share ideas to $^2$_____ a decision together. | In writing your view is fixed but by phone you can $^4$_____ it during the conversation. | They need to communicate with each $^6$_____ personally. |

**Functional language**

## Closing a deal

**1** Choose the correct option in italics.

**A:** OK, so I think we are close to a deal. As I [1]*understand / mean* it you need the fifty tablets delivered here by the end of September?

**B:** Not quite. We need the fifty tablets by the middle of September. We also need to train the staff to use them by the end of September.

**A:** OK, no problem. We can deliver them by September 18th.

**B:** That would be great. What is the price for those?

**A:** The best I can do is $650 each.

**B:** Including the apps we discussed?

**A:** That's normally a little more. Around $700 each.

**B:** What about training for our staff? How long would they need?

**A:** We are [2]*agreed / prepared* to give you five free training days for twenty-five employees. Each member of staff will need one day. So, you pay for twenty staff.

**B:** Could you do that between the 22nd and 29th?

**A:** No problem.

**B:** Good. So, we [3]*are agree / 've agreed* on the dates. That only [4]*leaves / means* the same point as before. Price.

**A:** So, what you [5]*agree / mean* is that you are happy with the tablet delivery dates and the training agreement, but you want a better price than $700? And you want the apps included?

**B:** I think that just about sums it [6]*up / in*, yes.

**A:** OK. I can agree to $670 per tablet. In [7]*return / sum*, we would need you to pay by the end of September. Are you able to do that?

**B:** [8]*If / When* it is as you say it is, we will be able to go ahead.

**A:** Agreed. Thank you very much.

## Talking about priorities

**2** Complete the comments made by a manager during a catch-up.

**1** Put it at the b _ _ _ _ _ of your list of things to do. It's really not important.

**2** It has to be done today. It's of u _ _ _ _ _ _ importance.

**3** Give it a h _ _ _ _ priority, please. It's pretty important.

**4** You can put it o _ _ for a while. It's not urgent.

**5** Don't waste t _ _ _ . Start it now.

**6** Put it in your s _ _ _ _ _ _ _ _ and do it when you have time.

**7** Could you make it your number one p _ _ _ _ _ _ _ _ ? Leave everything else.

**8** I know it's a bit of a d _ _ _ _ _ _ _ _ _ _ _ . You have so many other important things to do.

## Writing    Short report

**1A** Read the sentences from a report. Decide if they are part of the Introduction, Findings or Recommendations. Complete the table.

1
> The director has asked me to write this report to try to improve our performance at conferences.

2
> The managers should have three days off work to attend these courses. It is hoped these courses will be run off-site.

3
> It seems that staff do not feel confident in this soft skill, either in English or their own language.

4
> It is therefore recommended that we organise training courses in effective presentations and other communication skills. Our aims are to give the managers of the sales and marketing teams intensive courses as a priority, then train their staff.

5
> This report looks at reasons for these problems and aims to analyse why we are underperforming.

6
> One of the key problems is that staff do not have the communication skills needed. In fact, the first thing we noticed was that few of our staff give presentations at conferences.

7
> Finally, it will make recommendations.

8
> Recently, we have failed to make a good impression at these events compared to our competitors.

9
> It was found that staff were not prepared to do them because they have had no training in public speaking.

10
> We might therefore need to allocate extra budget for accommodation.

| Introduction | Findings | Recommendations |
|---|---|---|
|  |  |  |

**B** Put the sentences in Exercise 1A in the correct order.

**2** Read the situation below and think what recommendations you could make. Then write a report of about 160 words for the director.

> Your company has signed a contract with a Brazilian company, Media Sales BR. You have completed an audit of your technical and sales teams to identify potential issues in working with the new partner. It is important that employees in these departments have the language skills required to work in teams with the Brazilian company. Their technical team don't speak English at all, though their sales team members are fluent.
>
> The audit revealed that nobody in your technical team speaks Portuguese and only 70 percent of your overseas sales staff are fluent in English. You have three months before the contract starts.

- Introduce the report clearly, stating your reasons for writing it.
- State your findings clearly.
- Make realistic recommendations.

# Pronunciation

## Unit 1

### 1.1 Word stress

**1** Match the words (a–j) with the stress patterns (1–5).

1  Oo      _____  _____

2  Ooo     _____  _____

3  oO      _____  _____

4  oOo     _____  _____

5  ooOo    _____  _____

**a**  accountant      **f**  independence

**b**  ambitious       **g**  journalist

**c**  applied         **h**  movement

**d**  career          **i**  politician

**e**  confidence      **j**  problem

**2** ◀)P1.01 Listen and check. Then listen again and repeat the words.

**3** Write the stress pattern for these words, using *O* for the stressed syllable and *o* for the unstressed syllables.

1  ambition       _____          6  reliable        _____

2  dependable     _____          7  motivated       _____

3  determination  _____          8  organised       _____

4  flexibility    _____          9  passionate      _____

5  integrity      _____         10  resourcefulness _____

**4** ◀)P1.02 Listen and check. Then listen again and repeat the words.

### 1.2 Voice range

**1** ◀)P1.03 Listen to the sentences and tick (✔) the ones with a wide voice range.

1  I'm a recent graduate – I have a good degree. ☐

2  I can't even get an interview. ☐

3  I don't think there's anything on my profile that's special. ☐

4  How can I make myself stand out from the crowd? ☐

5  I created a website for one of my projects. ☐

6  That's really helpful. Thank you so much. ☐

7  It was useful … maybe a bit too useful. ☐

8  When I applied for six jobs, I got four interviews. ☐

9  And after four interviews, I got two job offers. ☐

10  That's the problem – I really can't decide. ☐

**2** Practise saying the sentences.

# Unit 2

## 2.2 Stress in compound nouns and noun phrases

**1** Choose the compound nouns and noun phrases which have a different stress pattern from the others.

1 **a** energy industry     **b** renewable energy     **c** tax deduction

2 **a** energy supply     **b** green energy     **c** oil company

3 **a** business sense     **b** design school     **c** future risk

4 **a** blog post     **b** job interview     **c** nightmare journey

5 **a** business partner     **b** long-term transition     **c** train station

**2** ◀)P2.01 Listen and check, then listen again and practise saying the compound nouns and noun phrases correctly.

**3** Practise saying these sentences.

1 Solar panels can reduce electricity bills.

2 To stop global warming and climate change, we have to cut emissions of greenhouse gases.

3 The energy industry still relies far too much on fossil fuels.

4 If there isn't a reliable energy supply, power cuts are inevitable.

**4** ◀)P2.02 Listen and check.

## 2.3 Stress in phrases for turn taking

**1** ◀)P2.03 Practise saying the sentences with the main stresses underlined.

1 <u>Yes</u>, do you have a <u>question</u>?

2 <u>What</u> did you want to <u>say</u>?

3 I'd <u>like</u> to make a <u>point</u> here if I <u>can</u>.

4 <u>Well</u>, if I could <u>just</u> <u>finish</u>, …

5 If I could <u>just</u> finish my <u>point</u>, …

6 <u>Sorry</u>, I <u>just</u> have <u>one</u> more thing to <u>say</u>.

7 <u>Can</u> I <u>just</u> <u>say</u> <u>something</u> here?

8 <u>Before</u> you <u>speak</u>, <u>let</u> me <u>just</u> <u>say</u> …

**2** Listen again and check, then listen again and practise.

## Unit 3

### 3.1 Stress in derived words

**1**  **P3.01 Listen to the sentences and underline the stressed syllable in the words below.**

1 movement

2 communication

3 construction

4 investigation

5 additional

6 presentation

7 reasonable

8 personal

9 happiness

10 detailed

**2 Listen again and practise saying the sentences.**

### 3.2 Weak forms in comparisons

**3 Before you listen, mark the words that you think will be spoken as weak forms.**

1 The Grand Canal took the longest to build.

2 The Suez Canal was more expensive than expected.

3 The Rhine has a width of more than half a kilometre in some places.

4 The Suez Canal was the most complicated project of the three.

5 The Panama team had to work a lot harder than the Suez team.

6 No other artificial waterway is as long or as old as the Grand Canal.

**2 P3.02 Listen and practise saying the sentences.**

# Unit 4

## 4.3 Pronunciation of -(e)s endings

**1** In each group of words, tick (✔) the word where the -(e)s ending adds an extra syllable.

| | | |
|---|---|---|
| 1 decides ☐ | manages ☐ | videos ☐ |
| 2 colleagues ☐ | differences ☐ | styles ☐ |
| 3 businesses ☐ | examples ☐ | managers ☐ |
| 4 copes ☐ | families ☐ | services ☐ |
| 5 agrees ☐ | experiences ☐ | factories ☐ |

**2** 🔊 P4.01 Listen and check, then listen again and practise saying the words.

**3** Practise saying these phrases.

1 apps for smartphones

2 advantages and disadvantages

3 choices and strategies

4 offices and factories

5 colleagues and families

6 examples of businesses

7 times of buses

8 clients' experiences

**4** 🔊 P4.02 Listen and check your pronunciation.

## 4.4 Consonant–vowel linking between words

**1** Before you listen, mark the likely consonant–vowel links in these sentences.

1 We want everyone to be involved in the conversation.

2 There's a lack of consensus in this group at the moment.

3 Did you find writing down your thoughts a good idea?

4 We should focus on ways of building consensus.

5 Think about group needs, not individual needs.

6 Everybody's opinion is of equal weight and is to be respected.

7 Well done everybody! It looks like everyone agrees.

8 No one in the group is more important than anyone else.

9 We can be much more efficient if we work in small groups.

10 The problem is that one or two people always dominate.

**2** 🔊 P4.03 Listen and check, then listen again and practise saying the sentences.

## Unit 5

### 5.1 Numbers of syllables in words

**1** In each group of words, tick (✔) the word which has a different number of syllables from the others.

| | | |
|---|---|---|
| 1 cashier ☐ | creating ☐ | patience ☐ |
| 2 precise ☐ | quality ☐ | social ☐ |
| 3 features ☐ | fuel ☐ | uses ☐ |
| 4 dependable ☐ | necessarily ☐ | unprecedented ☐ |
| 5 planned ☐ | prepared ☐ | received ☐ |
| 6 delivered ☐ | innovative ☐ | studying ☐ |
| 7 cafeteria ☐ | opportunity ☐ | ultimately ☐ |
| 8 fewer ☐ | ideas ☐ | styles ☐ |
| 9 accurate ☐ | clients ☐ | people ☐ |

**2** ◀)P5.01 Listen and check. Then listen again and practise saying the words.

**3** ◀)P5.02 Listen to the sentences. How many syllables do you hear in the underlined words?

1 I'll <u>probably</u> have a salad.  ____

2 In <u>general</u>, restaurants are using more technology.  ____

3 They might not hear your order <u>correctly</u>.  ____

4 Some people prefer a bit more social <u>interaction</u>.  ____

5 I <u>actually</u> think the quality's better.  ____

6 It's faster than a <u>traditional</u> restaurant.  ____

7 They're using really <u>powerful</u> technology.  ____

8 Look it up in your <u>dictionary</u>.  ____

**4** Practise saying the sentences.

### 5.2 Contrastive stress

**1** Before you listen, underline the two words in each sentence that you think will have contrastive stress.

1 He's already spent two hours in meetings and an hour writing emails.

2 He should be testing video games but he hasn't even looked at one today.

3 He looked for office jobs, but then a friend mentioned the games-testing job.

4 He applied for the job for a laugh, and was surprised when he got it.

5 When he got the job, his parents often asked, 'Have you found a real job yet?'

6 After three years in his first job, he left for a position with better pay.

7 When the company went out of business, he had to find a new job.

8 The money isn't great, but it's adequate.

**2** ◀)P5.03 Listen and check, then listen again and practise saying the sentences.

# Unit 6

## 6.2 Phrasing and pausing

**1** Before you listen, mark where you think there may be pauses in this presentation.

In today's competitive retail industry, security systems have to be more subtle and cost effective. However, they mustn't be so aggressive that it makes potential customers feel uncomfortable and lose the shop sales. Theft prevention has to stop thieves but mustn't frighten real shoppers.

With radio frequency ID chips, it is now possible to follow items and send instant alerts to security guards when these are moving towards the door. The retailer also needs to accept that theft is sometimes committed by staff. The solution doesn't need to be expensive or frightening for employees. Staff lockers with glass doors is one simple option.

**2** ◀ P6.01 Listen and check, then practise giving the presentation.

## 6.4 Stress in phrases

**1** Before you listen, mark where you think the two stresses will be in these phrases.

1 dealing with conflict

2 currently on vacation

3 see it from both sides

4 What do you suggest?

5 How do we proceed?

**2** ◀ P6.02 Listen and check, then listen again and practise saying the phrases.

**3** In each group of phrases, tick (✔) the one which has a different stress patterrn, with only *one* stress.

| | | |
|---|---|---|
| 1 that's fine with me ☐ | remain calm ☐ | management team ☐ |
| 2 tone of voice ☐ | review the situation ☐ | come to an agreement ☐ |
| 3 at the end of the week ☐ | look at the problem ☐ | currently on vacation ☐ |

**4** ◀ P6.03 Listen and check, then listen again and practise saying the phrases.

## Unit 7

### 7.2 Unstressed syllables at the end of a sentence

**1** 🔊 P7.01 **Listen and mark the main stress.**

1 How can I help you, Angela?

2 I can't hear you very well.

3 My internet connection isn't working.

4 I forgot to pay my mobile phone bill for last month.

**2 Practise saying the sentences.**

**3 Look at B's answers and mark where you think the main stress will be in each.**

1 **A:** It might work if you switch it off and back on again.

   **B:** I've already tried switching it off and back on again.

2 **A:** Have you raised this issue with your boss before?

   **B:** This is actually the third time I've raised it.

3 **A:** You need to press the red button.

   **B:** I can't see a red button.

4 **A:** Can I ask you for your phone number, please?

   **B:** But I've already told you what my phone number is.

**4** 🔊 P7.02 **Listen and check, then listen again and practise saying the sentences.**

### 7.4 Introducing a topic

**1** 🔊 P7.03 **Listen and underline the word with the main stress.**

1 in today's meeting

2 another way

3 the first thing we need to do

4 according to the manager

5 what we want to do

**2 Listen and check, then listen again and practise.**

**3** 🔊 P7.04 **Listen to B's answers. In the second half of B's responses, underline the word with the main stress.**

1 **A:** What's on the agenda for today?

   **B:** In today's meeting, we're going to brainstorm how to capture ideas.

2 **A:** How else can you do it?

   **B:** Another way is to use your smartphone.

3 **A:** What should our priority be?

   **B:** The first thing we need to do is to offer a good service.

4 **A:** Who has good ideas?

   **B:** According to the manager, we all have good ideas.

5 **A:** What do we want to do?

   **B:** What we want to do is make sure that we really think through the issues.

**4** 🔊 P7.05 **Listen and practise the full conversations.**

# Unit 8

## 8.2 Conditional sentences

**1** Underline the main stressed word in each part of these sentences.

1 If we held our meetings in a café, they'd feel less formal.

2 If she kept her office door open, she'd be easier to talk to.

3 If I wasn't so busy all the time, I'd get more work done!

4 They'd probably get more work done if they didn't chat so much.

5 If I were CEO, I'd give everyone a private office.

6 You'd know your colleagues better if you talked to them more.

7 Employees would be more productive if they had private offices to work in.

8 If you turned off your phone at six o'clock every night, your kids would be happier!

**2** ◀ P8.01 Listen and check, then listen again and practise the sentences.

## 8.5 Contractions in speech

**1** Rewrite the underlined words using contractions.

1 I <s>will not</s>  *won't*  be at work tomorrow, so I cannot _____ help you.

2 I could not _____ understand the instructions and I did not _____ know what to do.

3 The office furniture does not _____ look very attractive but it will _____ be OK for another year.

4 It seems that the problem has _____ been solved.

5 The order had not _____ been checked.

6 The company has _____ been taken over.

7 You must not _____ forget to update the stock records.

8 I would _____ like to make some recommendations, if you have _____ got time to meet.

**2** ◀ P8.02 Listen and check, then listen again and practise the sentences with contractions.

**3** ◀ P8.03 Listen and complete the conversation.

1 **A:** _____ been any problems, have there?

   **B:** Well, _____ been a few, actually.

2 **A:** Why _____ you just follow the instructions?

   **B:** _____ told you, I _____ understand them.

3 **A:** _____ heard that the company _____ taken over.

   **B:** The company _____ been taken over!

4 **A:** I hope the report _____ ready tomorrow.

   **B:** Don't worry, _____ be.

**4** Listen again and check, then listen again and practise the conversation.

## Unit 1

### Vocabulary

**1**
1 think outside the box
2 team player
3 communication skills
4 critical thinking
5 determination  6 set goals
7 can-do attitude  8 integrity

**2**
1 independent  2 passionate
3 confidence  4 motivation
5 resourceful  6 adaptability

**3**
1 depend**able**  2 flex**ible**
3 independ**ence**  4 enthus**iasm**
5 hon**est**  6 amb**ition**

### Grammar

**1**

| | Problem | Advice or suggestion |
|---|---|---|
| 1 | My computer skills are not very good. | You ought to go on a course. |
| 2 | I don't find my job very challenging. | Why not try speaking to your manager? |
| 3 | I really don't earn enough in my present job. | How about looking for a new one? |
| 4 | I've got too many online connections. | You shouldn't accept everybody. |
| 5 | My new job starts in three months. | Why don't you go travelling until then? |
| 6 | It takes me two hours to get to work. | You could apply for a transfer to another branch. |
| 7 | I get so nervous before interviews. | You should try thinking about something completely different. |

**2**  1 c  2 f  3 a  4 g
5 d  6 b  7 e

**3**  1 a  2 e  3 h  4 d
5 g  6 c  7 b  8 f

### Reading

**1**  1 F  2 F  3 DS  4 T  5 DS  6 T

**2**  1 sets the goals  2 harder
3 at the bottom  4 determined
5 can-do attitude  6 stand out

**3**  a honest

### Functional language

**1**
1 Do you know it?
2 How long were you in Abingdon for?
3 How long did you stay?
4 Where did you live exactly?
5 What did you do there?
6 Which places did you visit?
7 What did you like about it?

**2**  1 b  2 c  3 b

**3**
1 minute  2 appreciate
3 exciting  4 questions
5 explain  6 detail  7 call

### Writing

**1A**  Harry's email is formal. Emily's is informal.

**B**
1 Dear
2 I would like to introduce myself
3 Please feel free
4 I very much look forward to
5 Kind regards
6 I'm Emily Jones and
7 I was a
8 Perhaps we can meet up
9 Best wishes

**2**  See Exercise 1A for model answers.

## Unit 2

### Vocabulary

**1**
1 The tertiary ~~industry~~ sector includes education, public transport and financial services among others.
2 The ~~transportation~~ automotive industry is a difficult sector at the moment as fewer people are buying new cars.
3 I work in ~~manufacturing~~ retail. I manage a large supermarket outside Warsaw.
4 The largest part of the Australian economy is the ~~automotive~~ service sector, with tourism growing year on year.
5 The ~~oil~~ manufacturing industry is in decline in our country because it is cheaper to make goods abroad.
6 With so many goods moving around the world, companies in ~~fishing~~ transportation have great opportunities.

**2**  1 oil drilling  2 agriculture
3 metal extraction  4 cruise lines
5 health care  6 raw materials
7 construction  8 insurance

**3**  1 c (bank doesn't relate to tourism)
2 b (wine producing doesn't relate to extraction of raw material)
3 d (farm doesn't relate to manufacturing)
4 b (factory doesn't relate to retail)
5 c (robotics isn't a primary sector)
6 a (chemical plant doesn't relate to finance)
a 6  b 4  c 5  d 3  e 2  f 1

### Grammar

**1**  1 b  2 h  3 a  4 f  5 c  6 g
7 d  8 e

**2**  1 was talking  2 gave  3 joined
4 was working  5 went  6 had
7 were discussing  8 checked

**3**  1 When  2 was having  3 While
4 was listening  5 was driving
6 sent  7 While  8 called back
9 wanted  10 saw

### Listening

**1**  1 wind  2 on the land
3 economical  4 a lot of
5 cheaper  6 90 kph

**2**  1 F  2 T  3 T  4 F  5 T  6 F

**3**  1 energy  2 onshore / on the land
3 companies  4 windy
5 Efficiency  6 strong  7 France

### Functional language

**1**
1 ahead  2 continue  3 saying
4 interrupt  5 as  6 Excuse
7 thing  8 say  9 something
10 making  11 finish  12 speak

**2A**  1 Lalaurette  2 Sales department
3 G1964  4 451 644 753
5 time to speak  6 lunchtime

**B**  1 This is  2 spell
3 This is a message  4 contact
5 Could you  6 mobile
7 my number  8 send
9 get back to  10 look forward

### Writing

**1A**
1 pricing  2 slogan
3 May 31st  4 Organise
5 Kathy  6 Book venue
7 April 30th  8 Invite
9 Leona  10 June 10th

**B**  Yes: 1, 4, 5
No: 2, 3

**2  Model answer**
Dear colleagues,
We had a management meeting yesterday and decided to celebrate our tenth anniversary with a staff 'family and friends day'. The party will be on August 25th and before that we have a lot to do. Action points were agreed as follows:

| | | |
|---|---|---|
| Book venue | by June 30th | Carla and Pierre |
| Plan day | by July 15th | Belinda and Salvador |
| Book music | by July 21st | Felipe |
| Send invitations | by July 30th | Anna-Maria |
| Organise food | by August 10th | Sally and David |

We will be having a team meeting next week to go through the details.
Best wishes,

## Unit 3

### Vocabulary

**1**  1 d  2 c  3 a  4 f  5 e  6 b

**2**
1 schedule  2 Anticipate
3 milestones  4 budget
5 Setbacks  6 risk  7 register
8 manager

**3**
1 construction  2 addition
3 attachment  4 investigated
5 solution
6 identity / identification
7 moving  8 management

### Grammar

**1**
1 oldest  2 expensive  3 higher
4 longer  5 most spectacular
6 scariest  7 tallest
8 most amazing

**2** 1 most beautiful
2 busiest
3 longer
4 high
5 most expensive
6 biggest
7 heaviest
8 most complex

## Reading

**1** 1 £14.8 billion  2 2009  3 2018
4 45 minutes  5 200 million
6 42 km  7 1,500 passengers
8 10 percent / 10%  9 55,000
10 75,000

**2** 1 c  2 c  3 c  4 b  5 a  6 a

## Functional language

**1** 1 bring me up to speed
2 no room for manoeuvre
3 can't compromise
4 My hands are tied
5 can certainly do that
6 You need to meet
7 leave it with me

**2** 1 doing  2 happening  3 latest
4 Where  5 update  6 finish
7 impediment  8 follow

## Writing

**1** 1 b  2 a  3 d  4 c  5 f  6 e

**2** **Model answer**
Dear Jason,
I hope you are well. It was good to
catch up last Thursday at the project
meeting. By the way, I know you're
busy, but I need your help with
a presentation to HR next week.
Could you let me have the following
information?
I'd like to know if the third phase of
the China project is now complete.
If not, what date do you have for
completion? Is Emilia now working
on the project? I'd appreciate it if
you could give me her starting date.
Sorry to ask so many questions!
Would you mind sending me the
latest schedule for the project?
Would it be possible to have this
information by tomorrow?
I'd also like to request a meeting
with the customer in Hong Kong in
April. I'd therefore be grateful if you
could contact him and arrange it.
Thanks in advance.
Kind regards,

## Unit 4

## Vocabulary

**1** 1 marketing strategy
2 product customisation
3 target territories
4 consumer brands
5 local preferences
6 luxury goods

**2** 1 prefer  2 produced  3 standard
4 preferences  5 customisation
6 adaptable

**3** 1 appealing  2 consumers
3 production  4 customised
5 specialises  6 growth  7 target

## Grammar

**1** 1 was launched  2 runs
3 was built  4 are made
5 recommended  6 were given
7 were diverted  8 is thought

**2** 1 are connected  2 was founded
3 grew  4 was bought
5 were merged  6 say
7 translates  8 are booked

**3** 1 was the company founded?
2 grew  3 were they bought
4 paid  5 were they merged
6 are its webpages translated

## Listening

**1** 1 a  2 b

**2** 1 T  2 T  3 F  4 T  5 T  6 F
7 T  8 F

**3** 1 salesman (called Herman Lay)
2 1961  3 PepsiCo
4 the UK and Ireland  5 logo
6 flavour  7 social media
8 young  9 brand  10 strategy

## Functional language

**1** 1 move  2 good  3 moment
4 reminds  5 plenty  6 come
7 forget  8 should

**2** 1 not sure I agree / afraid I disagree
2 afraid I disagree / not sure I agree
3 right  4 should
5 don't agree with
6 Why don't we  7 Good idea
8 not a bad idea  9 How about if

## Writing

**1** 1 d  2 f  3 c  4 a
5 g  6 e  7 b

**2** **Model answer**
Dear Sirs,
We are writing to you to confirm
your order number IX765 for 80
model PWB2 desk lamps, which we
received last week.
As agreed on the telephone when we
talked about your order, I confirm we
will deliver the goods on 5th May
to your Perth office at a price of $40
per unit. We discussed a discount of
20 percent providing you order 80
or more and you will be pleased to
know that this is included in the final
price of $3,200.
As a new customer, your payment
terms are 30 days after the invoice
date and we enclose full terms and
conditions for your records. I also
enclose a new catalogue. The
delivery address is BRF, 12, Tristram
Street, Perth.
We thank you for your business and
look forward to working with you. If
you have any queries, please do not
hesitate to contact us.
Yours faithfully,

## Unit 5

## Vocabulary

**1** 1 disrupt  2 magical  3 choice
4 customise  5 interacting
6 place  7 swipe  8 automated

**2** 1 stylish  2 top-of-the-range
3 dependable  4 classic
5 unique  6 well designed

**3** 1 classic, unique
2 stylish, innovative
3 top-of-the-range, well designed,
advanced
4 user-friendly, dependable

## Grammar

**1** 1 I have just ordered a new
smartphone.
2 We have already interviewed
three candidates.
3 Have you had lunch yet?
4 I have already booked my ticket.
5 Have you found a solution yet?
6 I started two hours ago but
I haven't finished yet.
7 I am afraid we have already
discussed that point.
8 I am sorry but she has just left.

**2** 1 d  2 e  3 g  4 b  5 h  6 a
7 f  8 c

**3** 1 yet, just  2 already  3 yet

## Listening

**1** 1 b  2 c  3 b  4 c  5 c  6 c
7 b  8 a

**2** 1 luxury  2 safely  3 dependable
4 bad  5 assurance  6 standard
7 solutions  8 meal

## Functional language

**1** 1 mean  2 get  3 Is  4 do
5 take  6 think  7 Tell  8 is/'s

**2** 1 measures  2 weighs  3 means
4 in  5 of  6 means  7 with
8 lets

## Writing

**1A** 1 chose  2 said  3 decided
4 What  5 impressed
6 particularly  7 downside
8 Another  9 thing

**B** **reasons for buying:** good price,
good reviews
**Good points:** size, lights, sound
quality
**Bad points:** battery life, case,
instructions, technical issues
**Conclusion:** two-star rating

**2** **Model answer**
I decided to buy a tablet to watch
films when travelling. My colleague
had one like this and I also read a
lot of reviews before choosing this
one. The price is very good, at least
25 percent cheaper than other
brands. It seems good value for
money. I was impressed by the size
of the screen, and it is very easy
to use. Another good thing is the
graphics which are very clear.

I have used it a lot and am reasonably happy.
However, there are one or two negatives. One of the things I don't like is the volume. It is not very loud, even when I wear headphones. Another problem is the battery life, which is only three hours. Also, the screen gets dirty very easily!
In conclusion, I think I should have bought a more expensive tablet. I can only give this product three stars.

# Unit 6

## Vocabulary

**1** **1** issued **2** handle **3** pose
**4** hold **5** fitted **6** record

**2** **1** high-visibility clothing
**2** steel toe-cap boots
**3** ear defenders
**4** cut-resistant gloves
**5** face mask
**6** hard hat
**7** goggles

**3** **1** hurt **2** slipped **3** fell **4** cut
**5** dropped **6** broke **7** hit
**8** damaged **9** bleed **10** injured

## Grammar

**1** **1** g **2** h **3** a **4** f **5** c **6** e
**7** b **8** d

**2** **1** must **2** mustn't **3** mustn't
**4** have to **5** must **6** don't have to
**7** needs to **8** has to **9** must
**10** don't need to

**3** **1** don't have to **2** didn't need to
**3** mustn't **4** has to **5** have to
**6** had to

## Reading

**1** **1** D **2** A **3** E **4** C **5** B

**2** **1** workers **2** their families
**3** police **4** Hackers
**5** their employees **6** careers

**3** **1** steal **2** leave **3** robbery
**4** equipment **5** private
**6** prisons **7** monitor **8** fraud

## Functional language

**1** **1** It's great that you
**2** I understand that
**3** it's a question of
**4** we really appreciate all
**5** My position is
**6** we can't agree unless
**7** needs signing
**8** has to be

**2** **2** k **3** e **4** a **5** h **6** b **7** g
**8** i **9** f **10** d **11** j

## Writing

**1** **DOs**
Report any faulty equipment to your manager.
Follow safety instructions carefully.
You must wear your name badge at all times.

**DON'Ts**
No one is permitted to use technical equipment without training.
You are not allowed to eat while working.
Don't remove company property.
**WARNINGS**
Watch out for wet floors.
Be careful not to damage company equipment.

**2** **Model answer**
GENERAL INSTRUCTIONS FOR HEALTH, SAFETY AND FITNESS AT WORK
Health
- Don't come to work if you're ill. You must stay at home until you feel better.
- Beware of flu. Wash your hands regularly to help avoid bacteria.
- No one is permitted to use the air conditioning in the winter as the air spreads illness.
Safety
- Make sure you sit at the correct height when you are using your monitor.
- You're not allowed to repair company equipment yourself. Report any problems to IT – call 4343 to log a maintenance request.
Fitness
- Try the healthy restaurant options.
- Take the stairs instead of the lift.
- Go for a walk at lunchtime if you can't exercise.
- Make use of the company's private healthcare. Don't forget to book your annual appointment with the nurse.

# Unit 7

## Vocabulary

**1** **1** boarding **2** 'no-frills'
**3** class **4** premium **5** attention
**6** treatment

**2** **1** satisfied **2** helpful **3** anxious
**4** assistance **5** demanding
**6** requested **7** apologised
**8** empathy **9** handled
**10** confident

**3** **1** The passenger was probably anxious about take-off.
**2** A lot of people aren't confident about flying.
**3** Unfortunately, nobody offered assistance to the anxious passenger.
**4** The flight attendant didn't apologise to the passengers for the delay.
**5** Neither of the passengers was satisfied with the service.

## Grammar

**1** **1** c **2** f **3** e **4** b **5** d **6** a

**2** **1** meeting **2** losing **3** changing
**4** to realise **5** to reduce
**6** to meet up

**3** **1** to book **2** using **3** to write
**4** to call **5** to waste **6** to stay

## Reading

**1** Julia ✗ Roberto ✔

**2** **1** F **2** T **3** F **4** T **5** F **6** T

**3** **1** b **2** b **3** c **4** b

## Functional language

**1** **1** has filled me in on the
**2** your side of things
**3** has told me about that
**4** correct about that
**5** I'll go through
**6** Please, understand that I see
**7** we'll come up with a
**8** Let me
**9** I'm sure

**2** **1** The first thing we need to do
**2** Our team came up with the idea of
**3** Our team would like to push the idea of
**4** We suggest everyone needs to
**5** The thing is, it's got to be

## Writing

**1A** **1** d **2** b **3** e **4** g **5** f
**6** c **7** a

**B**

| Beginning | Details | Closing |
|---|---|---|
| d | b, e, g | f, c, a |

**2** **Model answer**
Dear Diana,
I am writing to thank you for the brochure you recently designed for our 10th anniversary.
It was a beautiful design and we were very pleased with it. I wanted you to know how much we appreciated all your hard work, and the creativity of both you and your team. We would also like to express our appreciation for the patience you showed when we sent you those extra photos at the last minute! The price we agreed for the project was really good value, as we can see from the final version. Throughout the project, Velleda, your designer, was really patient and professional.
We will certainly use your company again in the future and have already recommended you to other companies and our professional association.
Thanks again,
Bruce

# Unit 8

## Vocabulary

**1** **1** check **2** Catch up on **3** Reply
**4** internal **5** master **6** overload

**2** 1 overload  2 internal  3 check
4 catch up  5 reply  6 mastered

**3** 1 improve  2 engaged  3 choice
4 concentrate  5 productive
6 encourage

## Grammar

**1** 1 e  2 d  3 b  4 c  5 a

**2** 1 f  2 d  3 a  4 e  5 c  6 b

**3** 1 will  2 wouldn't  3 didn't
4 won't  5 might  6 doesn't
7 don't

## Listening

**1** 1 e  2 c  3 b  4 d  5 a

**2** 1 a  2 b  3 c  4 c  5 b  6 c

**3** 1 nothing  2 make  3 way
4 change  5 decisions
6 employee

## Functional language

**1** 1 understand  2 prepared
3 've agreed  4 leaves  5 mean
6 up  7 return  8 If

**2** 1 bottom  2 utmost  3 high
4 off  5 time  6 schedule
7 priority  8 distraction

## Writing

**1A** **Introduction:** 1, 5, 7, 8
**Findings:** 3, 6, 9
**Recommendations:** 2, 4, 10

**B** 1, 8, 5, 7 / 6, 9, 3 / 4, 2, 10

**2** **Model answer**
Introduction
The director has asked me to
write this report to try to identify
potential issues working with our
partner – the Brazilian company,
Media Sales BR. This report looks at
the results of a recent audit of our
sales and technical teams. Finally,
it will make recommendations.
Findings
It was found that only 70 percent
of our overseas sales staff speak
fluent English and none of the
technical team speaks Portuguese.
One of the key problems is these
teams will need to work in these
languages with our Brazilian
colleagues in three months' time.
Recommendations
It is therefore recommended
that we organise on-site training
courses in English and Portuguese.
Our aims are to train all members
of the technical team in Portuguese
and provide English classes for some
overseas sales staff.
The managers of these teams
should have three weeks off work
to attend full-time, intensive
courses. It is hoped these courses
will be run in the US and Brazil.
We might therefore need to
allocate extra budget for flights
and accommodation.

# Pronunciation

## Unit 1
### 1.1

**1**
| | | | |
|---|---|---|---|
| 1 | Oo | movement | problem |
| 2 | Ooo | confidence | journalist |
| 3 | oO | applied | career |
| 4 | oOo | accountant | ambitious |
| 5 | ooOo | politician | independence |

**3**
| | | |
|---|---|---|
| 1 | ambition | oOo |
| 2 | dependable | oOoo |
| 3 | determination | oooOo |
| 4 | flexibility | ooOoo |
| 5 | integrity | oOoo |
| 6 | reliable | oOoo |
| 7 | motivated | Oooo |
| 8 | organised | Ooo |
| 9 | passionate | Ooo |
| 10 | resourcefulness | oOoo |

### 1.2

**1** 1 I'm a recent graduate – I have a
good degree. ✔
2 I can't even get an interview. ✔
3 I don't think there's anything on
my profile that's special.
4 How can I make myself stand
out from the crowd? ✔
5 I created a website for one of
my projects. ✔
6 That's really helpful. Thank you
so much. ✔
7 It was useful … maybe a bit too
useful.
8 When I applied for six jobs, I got
four interviews. ✔
9 And after four interviews, I got
two job offers. ✔
10 That's the problem – I really
can't decide.

## Unit 2
### 2.2

**1** 1 **b** renewable <u>energy</u>
2 **b** green <u>energy</u>
3 **c** future <u>risk</u>
4 **c** nightmare <u>journey</u>
5 **b** long-term tran<u>sition</u>

## Unit 3
### 3.1

**1** 1 <u>move</u>ment
2 communi<u>ca</u>tion
3 con<u>struc</u>tion
4 investi<u>ga</u>tion
5 ad<u>di</u>tional
6 presen<u>ta</u>tion
7 <u>rea</u>sonable
8 <u>per</u>sonal
9 <u>happi</u>ness
10 <u>de</u>tailed

### 3.2

**1** 1 <u>The</u> Grand Canal took <u>the</u>
longest <u>to</u> build.
2 <u>The</u> Suez Canal <u>was</u> more
expensive <u>than</u> expected.
3 <u>The</u> Rhine has <u>a</u> width <u>of</u> more <u>than</u>
half <u>a</u> kilometre in some places.

4 <u>The</u> Suez Canal <u>was the</u> most
complicated project <u>of the</u> three.
5 <u>The</u> Panama team had <u>to</u> work
<u>a</u> lot harder <u>than the</u> Suez team.
6 No other artificial waterway is <u>as</u>
long or <u>as</u> old <u>as the</u> Grand Canal.

## Unit 4
### 4.3

**1** 1 manages
2 differences
3 businesses
4 services
5 experiences

### 4.4

**1** 1 We want‿everyone to be
involved‿in the conversation.
2 There's a lack‿of consensus‿in
this group‿at the moment.
3 Did you find writing down your
thoughts‿a good idea?
4 We should focus‿on ways‿of
building consensus.
5 Think‿about group needs,
not‿individual needs.
6 Everybody's‿opinion‿is‿of‿
‿equal weight‿and‿is to be
respected.
7 Well done‿everybody! It looks
like‿everyone‿agrees.
8 No one‿in the group‿is more‿
‿important than‿anyone‿else.
9 We can be much more‿efficient‿
‿if we work‿in small groups.
10 The problem‿is that one‿or
two people‿always dominate.

## Unit 5
### 5.1

**1** 1 creating
2 quality
3 fuel
4 dependable
5 planned
6 innovative
7 ultimately
8 styles
9 accurate

**3** 1 two syllables
2 two syllables
3 two syllables
4 three syllables
5 two syllables
6 three syllables
7 two syllables
8 three syllables

### 5.2

**1** 1 He's already spent two hours in
<u>meetings</u> and an hour writing
<u>emails</u>.
2 He should be <u>testing</u> video games
but he hasn't even <u>looked</u> at one
today.
3 He looked for <u>office</u> jobs, but then
a friend mentioned the <u>games-
testing</u> job.
4 He applied for the job for a <u>laugh</u>,
and was surprised when he <u>got</u> it.

5 When he <u>got</u> the job, his parents often asked, 'Have you found a <u>real</u> job yet?'

6 After three years in his <u>first</u> job, he left for a position with better <u>pay</u>.

7 When the company went out of <u>business</u>, he had to find a <u>new</u> job.

8 The money isn't <u>great</u>, but it's <u>adequate</u>.

## Unit 6

### 6.2

**1** In today's competitive retail industry, / security systems have to be more subtle / and cost effective. / However, / they mustn't be so aggressive that it makes potential customers feel uncomfortable / and lose the shop sales. / Theft prevention has to stop thieves / but mustn't frighten real shoppers.
With radio frequency ID chips, / it is now possible to follow items / and send instant alerts to security guards / when these are moving towards the door. / The retailer also needs to accept / that theft is sometimes committed by staff. / The solution doesn't need to be expensive / or frightening for employees. / Staff lockers with glass doors is one simple option.

### 6.4

**1**
1 <u>dea</u>ling with <u>c</u>onflict
2 <u>currently on vacation</u>
3 <u>see</u> it from <u>both</u> sides
4 <u>What</u> do you su<u>ggest</u>?
5 <u>How</u> do we pro<u>ceed</u>?

**3**
1 <u>management</u> team
2 re<u>view</u> the situation
3 <u>look</u> at the problem

## Unit 7

### 7.2

**1**
1 How can I <u>help</u> you, Angela?
2 I can't <u>hear</u> you very well.
3 My <u>internet</u> connection isn't working.
4 I forgot to pay my mobile <u>phone</u> bill for last month.

**3**
1 I've already <u>tried</u> switching it off and back on again.
2 This is actually the <u>third</u> time I've raised it.
3 I can't <u>see</u> a red button.
4 But I've already <u>told</u> you what my phone number is.

### 7.4

**1**
1 in <u>today's</u> meeting
2 <u>another</u> way
3 the <u>first</u> thing we need to do
4 according to the <u>manager</u>
5 what we want to <u>do</u>

**3**
1 In today's meeting, we're going to brainstorm how to capture <u>ideas</u>.
2 Another way is to use your <u>smartphone</u>.
3 The first thing we need to do is to offer a good <u>service</u>.
4 According to the manager, we <u>all</u> have good ideas.
5 What we want to do is make sure that we really think <u>through</u> the issues.

## Unit 8

### 8.2

**1**
1 If we held our meetings in a <u>café</u>, they'd feel less <u>formal</u>.
2 If she kept her office <u>door</u> open, she'd be easier to <u>talk</u> to.
3 If I wasn't so <u>busy</u> all the time, I'd get more <u>work</u> done!
4 They'd probably get more <u>work</u> done if they didn't <u>chat</u> so much.
5 If I were <u>CEO</u>, I'd give everyone a private <u>office</u>.
6 You'd know your colleagues <u>better</u> if you <u>talked</u> to them more.
7 Employees would be more <u>productive</u> if they had private <u>offices</u> to work in.
8 If you turned off your phone at six o'<u>clock</u> every night, your kids would be <u>happier</u>!

### 8.5

**1**
1 I <u>won't</u> be at work tomorrow, so I <u>can't</u> help you.
2 I <u>couldn't</u> understand the instructions and I <u>didn't</u> know what to do.
3 The office furniture <u>doesn't</u> look very attractive but <u>it'll</u> be OK for another year.
4 It seems that the <u>problem's</u> been solved.
5 The order <u>hadn't</u> been checked.
6 The <u>company's</u> been taken over.
7 You <u>mustn't</u> forget to update the stock records.
8 <u>I'd</u> like to make some recommendations, if <u>you've</u> got time to meet.

**3**
1 There haven't, there have
2 didn't, I've, couldn't
3 We've, 's been, has not
4 'll be, it will

# Audioscripts

🔊 2.01

**A** = Anna  **J** = John  **M** = Maria

**A:** Good evening. My name's Anna Barclay. Welcome to Green Business, the business and environment podcast. Today, we're going to be discussing an important source of energy – wind power. I have two guests – one from the UK and one from New Zealand. John Preston works for a UK company which built and now manages a number of offshore windfarms, that is windfarms where the turbines are located at sea. Good evening, John.

**J:** Good evening, Anna.

**A:** My second guest is Maria Taupo, from New Zealand. She's involved with an onshore windfarm, one of the first that was built on a real farm, rather than at sea. Good evening Maria.

**M:** Good evening Anna.

**A:** So, my first question is simple. John, why do we want to generate power from the wind?

**J:** Well, obviously the main advantage of wind power is that it's completely renewable. Wind comes and goes all the time. In the UK, a number of energy companies are getting into the wind power business.

**A:** That sounds interesting. Is it economical?

**J:** It's more economical than it was but you still need regular wind.

**A:** And is that why you're building them in New Zealand, Maria?

**M:** Yes, exactly. New Zealand is a very windy country. About twenty years ago, wind power was an obvious idea but we didn't really have the technology then, but now we have, it's easy and the benefits are obvious.

**A:** I see. So, how efficient is wind power? John?

**J:** We're improving efficiency every year. Our company started building windfarms about ten years ago and at first, they weren't very efficient. But now, a turbine generates twice as much electricity as it did then. This development means that the price of electricity can go down, which is good for the UK customer.

**A:** People say that windfarms are not always active. Is that true?

**M:** Not really. Our turbines turn in wind as low as 14 kph and as strong as 90 kph. In any wind stronger than that, they'd turn too fast and become dangerous, so they automatically stop turning.

**A:** I see. So, the UK and New Zealand are leaders in this sort of energy business?

**M:** Definitely and it'll continue to grow.

**A:** Can you export the knowledge?

**J:** Of course. UK companies already have projects in the USA, France and Germany. The Americans are now interested in windfarms at sea, too. Before they were only interested in windfarms onshore – that is great business for us. I think the possibilities for both the onshore and the offshore wind industry are huge.

**M:** I agree. New Zealand is now one of the leaders in windfarm technology. Thirty years ago, we were worrying about oil supplies. Now, fossil fuels are less important.

**A:** Thanks very much. I'd like to introduce another guest now who disagrees with you …

🔊 2.02

This is Morgane Lalaurette. I'll spell that for you: L-A-L-A-U-R-E-double T-E. This is a message for Julio Casas in your Sales department. You asked me to contact you to discuss order G1964, which I'm still waiting for. Could you call me back on my mobile? In case you don't have my number, I'm on 08451 644 753. Or can you send me an email so we can fix another time to speak? I really need this delivery as soon as possible. Could you get back to me by lunchtime tomorrow? Thanks a lot. I look forward to hearing from you.

🔊 2.03

**L** = Leona  **J** = Jack  **K** = Kathy

**L:** It's been a great meeting. Thanks for your excellent presentation, Jack.

**J:** Thanks, Leona. I'm glad you enjoyed it.

**L:** And Kathy, thanks for coming. I know you had to get up early this morning to get here on time.

**K:** No problem, Leona.

**L:** So, let's just finish off with the action points. The first point was the new pricing for the range. I think we agreed we needed that by July 1st.

**J:** That's correct. Neither Kathy nor I can do that. That's one for you, Leona.

**L:** OK. New pricing. I'll need to talk to the Finance Director. Now, the next one was the new slogan. Any thoughts?

**J:** I'm happy to do that. I can get the marketing team to help. When do you need it by?

**L:** What did we say? We want the final design for the campaign in September so the end of the month for the slogan if that's OK, Jack?

**J:** That's fine. Put May 31st on the action points.

**L:** OK. May 31st. Jack. Kathy? Can you organise social media? We want things happening by the end of August so you'll need everything ready two weeks before. Let's say August 15th.

**K:** That's OK. Is there anything else to do? What about the launch event?

**L:** Oh … yes. We need to have that in September. Somewhere a bit different. How about a museum or an art gallery?

**K:** Put my name down for that and I'll start looking. There are some good possibilities if we book early.

**L:** Perfect. Try and book it by April 30th. They all get booked up so quickly. So that's Kathy. Book venue. April 30th.

**J:** Who are we going to invite? It'll be an important part of the campaign.

**L:** I'll discuss that with the CEO and get invitations out by early June. Say June 10th. Leona. Invitations. June 10th. OK. I think we've covered everything. Thanks again for all your hard work. Have we got time for lunch?

🔊 4.01

Good morning and welcome to my presentation. I'm a little nervous because it's my first this wyear. My subject as part of the Globalisation module for this semester is from the food industry. I've chosen a company which makes snacks. I'm going to be looking at one of the most widely eaten snacks in the world – what the Americans call the potato chip, and what people in the UK call the potato crisp. I have studied one of the market leaders and particularly how they have been using social media to customise their offer to different regions depending on local preferences. I'm happy to take any questions at the end. Lay's has been around since 1932 when it was started by a salesman called Herman Lay. In 1961, it merged with a company called Frito to become Frito-Lay and then four years later with Pepsi Cola to form PepsiCo which is the current parent company name. From then on Lay's became a truly international crisp brand. Interestingly, for such a global brand Lay's don't always use that name. In the UK and Ireland, for example, they acquired Walkers Crisps in 1989 and continue to use that name to this day. The logo, on the other hand, is the Lay's logo with the Walkers' name on it. It is worth noting that in a global world a logo is often more memorable than a name – think of McDonald's golden arches or the Nike swoosh. In different parts of the world though a brand name can have more value. The name of our university, for example, is well-known all over the world.

So how does such a huge company with market leadership in so many countries all over the world use social media? One of their biggest successes has been their 'Choose a flavour' campaign, where the general public are asked to invent a new flavour for the crisps. Lay's have done regional campaigns in the UK, Australia and the USA among others, and the results are amazing.

Each year the number of customers involved gets larger. Lay's use Facebook, Twitter and other social media to have a series of conversations with their customers. Ultimately, this leads to what the consumer and the producer want, a new product and a lot of talk about the brand.

Customers are asked to suggest new flavours, and during the campaign the new ideas are discussed by other consumers through social media. A short list is produced and samples of the new flavours are made up. Tens of thousands of people give their opinions before a final decision is made and the new flavour is launched. This sort of campaign is aimed at a young audience. It improves knowledge of the brand and gives a role to loyal customers. All in all, it is a very good marketing strategy for the 21st century. I hope you enjoyed my presentation. Now, if any one has any questions I will happily answer them. If not, I will hand over to my classmate Hirumi for her presentation.

🔊 5.01

**I** = Interviewer  **S** = Steven Walker
**P** = Penny Tranter

**I:** Welcome again to *The World at Work*. Today we're going to be talking to people with some of the best jobs in the world – product testers. They get the chance to try food, clothes, make-up or gadgets long before the rest of us. I have two guests with me, both of whom spend a lot of time testing. My first guest is Steven Walker. Good evening, Steven. What is your job?

**S:** I'm a luxury car test driver.

**I:** Wow. Is that a full-time position?

**S:** Yes, it is. I work for a major car company and my job is to try out the new cars.

**I:** How did you get the job?

**S:** I was already with the company working as an engineer. I've always wanted to be a test driver since I was at school so when our test driver retired, I applied for the job.

**I:** And what do you do exactly?

**S:** I drive the cars on our own circuit and check that they work well and safely.

**I:** What sort of things do you check?

**S:** Everything. These cars are top-of-the-range so they need to be very comfortable, very fast and very dependable. I need to make sure you can use all the equipment and drive safely. I also need to check that they are easy to drive in bad weather.

**I:** Do you ever have accidents?

**S:** Not very often. Actually, the last one was useful because we then changed a couple of things to make the car even safer!

**I:** I suppose you can't keep the car after testing?

**S:** Unfortunately, not. They haven't let me keep one yet! I drive home in my boring old family car.

**I:** Thanks, Steven. My other guest is Penny Tranter. What do you test, Penny?

**P:** My job is a dream job. I test food!

**I:** So, you work in a kitchen?

**P:** Not exactly. I work in quality assurance for a restaurant chain. I don't actually cook at all but I test it to see if it tastes right. I'm very good at tasting flavours but I'm actually not very good at cooking! In fact, at home my husband always does the cooking.

**I:** And this is a full-time job?

**P:** Yes. They use me when they're developing new dishes and to check the food in our restaurants. I make sure it is up to standard.

**I:** So, what do you do?

**P:** Well, with new dishes I'm involved at all stages from the idea to the final dish. As I said, I don't cook. We start with a prototype and ask a group of people to eat it and comment. We take the feedback and our group of chefs develop the best possible dish. When it is finally on sale, I will then test it to make sure it is the same everywhere. I spend a lot of time on the road going to our different restaurants.

**I:** And if there is a problem?

**P:** I call my boss and we try to find a solution. But that rarely happens.

**I:** Do the chefs recognise you when you arrive at their restaurant?

**P:** Of course. I know them all. But a few times each year, I send mystery shoppers.

**I:** Who are they?

**P:** Just normal, average people. We offer them free meals in return for an honest report about our food.

**I:** That sounds interesting. How do I apply?

🔊 8.01

**I** = Interviewer  **A** = Andreas

**I:** Welcome to our podcast, *Three Questions With*. Today's guest is Andreas Hammer, a communications expert. Welcome, Andreas.

**A:** Hello.

**I:** My first question is for people looking for their first job after school or university. What communication skills do young people need to develop when they start working?

**A:** That's a very good question. Speaking is a key communication skill but in fact the first thing we all need to do is to remember that

it is OK to say nothing at first. Take time to think when someone asks you a question. And if you're not sure you've understood, check. For example, if I'm not clear what information you're asking for with one of your questions, I'll ask you to repeat it. Sometimes in meetings nobody knows the answer. The worst thing to do is to act like an eager student and answer immediately. I see a lot of clever people who always had the answer at school or college who still want to be the first to answer at work. If I were them, I would say nothing. Quiet people, on the other hand, need to be encouraged to offer ideas because in meetings we usually arrive at answers and make decisions by sharing lots of different opinions. We can only decide after a lot of discussion.

**I:** So how should young professionals communicate at work?

**A:** Compared with school or university, the workplace is more formal. I know some companies have a relaxed dress code but you still have to use the right language with the right person. If you aren't sure, choose formal. You must also find the right way to communicate. Sometimes you can have a casual conversation by the water-cooler but at other times you need a more formal meeting. Using the phone or sending an email are also very different ways of communication and it is important to make the right choice. If you're not sure, use the phone. On the phone, you can change your view as you talk. If you send an email, it will be too late to change. Your opinion is fixed.

**I:** That's a good point. Finally, what about managers? What communication skills does a good manager need?

**A:** We often describe people as good communicators. Managers have to be the best communicators. They are often in the middle between the directors making decisions and the staff having to do what has been decided. A good manager must communicate the sense of the decision in a way the employee understands it personally. Explaining and illustrating for each individual – that's good communication.

**I:** Andreas Hammer. Thanks very much.

## 1.1 Word stress

🔊 P1.01

1 movement  problem
2 confidence  journalist
3 applied  career
4 accountant  ambitious
5 politician  independence

🔊 P1.02

ambition  dependable
determination  flexibility
integrity  reliable  motivated
organised  passionate
resourcefulness

## 1.2 Voice range

🔊 P1.03

1 I'm a recent graduate – I have a good degree.
2 I can't even get an interview.
3 I don't think there's anything on my profile that's special.
4 How can I make myself stand out from the crowd?
5 I created a website for one of my projects.
6 That's really helpful. Thank you so much.
7 It was useful … maybe a bit too useful.
8 When I applied for six jobs, I got four interviews.
9 And after four interviews, I got two job offers.
10 That's the problem – I really can't decide.

## 2.1 Stress in compound nouns and noun phrases

🔊 P2.01

1 energy industry, renewable energy, tax deduction
2 energy supply, green energy, oil company
3 business sense, design school, future risk
4 blog post, job interview, nightmare journey
5 business partner, long-term transition, train station

🔊 P2.02

1 Solar panels can reduce electricity bills.
2 To stop global warming and climate change, we have to cut emissions of greenhouse gases.
3 The energy industry still relies far too much on fossil fuels.
4 If there isn't a reliable energy supply, power cuts are inevitable.

## 2.3 Stress in phrases for turn taking

🔊 P2.03

1 Yes, do you have a question?
2 What did you want to say?
3 I'd like to make a point here if I can.
4 Well, if I could just finish, …
5 If I could just finish my point, …
6 Sorry, I just have one more thing to say.
7 Can I just say something here?
8 Before you speak, let me just say …

## 3.1 Stress in derived words

🔊 P3.01

1 The problem was caused by people reacting to the movement of the bridge.
2 One immediate priority for project managers is to ensure clear communication.
3 The construction of the bridge required more time and money than anticipated.
4 The engineers closed the bridge to conduct an investigation.
5 They fixed the problem by attaching additional parts.
6 The biggest challenge was the presentation.
7 Do you think this was a reasonable length of time?
8 Everyone should have a personal budget.
9 Controlling your money is the key to financial happiness.
10 Some people say having a detailed schedule increases stress.

## 3.2 Weak forms in comparisons

🔊 P3.02

1 The Grand Canal took the longest to build.
2 The Suez Canal was more expensive than expected.
3 The Rhine has a width of more than half a kilometre in some places.
4 The Suez Canal was the most complicated project of the three.
5 The Panama team had to work a lot harder than the Suez team.
6 No other artificial waterway is as long or as old as the Grand Canal.

## 4.3 Pronunciation of -(e)s endings

🔊 P4.01

1 decides, manages, videos
2 colleagues, differences, styles
3 businesses, examples, managers
4 copes, families, services
5 agrees, experiences, factories

🔊 P4.02

1 apps for smartphones
2 advantages and disadvantages
3 choices and strategies
4 offices and factories
5 colleagues and families
6 examples of businesses
7 times of buses
8 clients' experiences

## 4.4 Consonant–vowel linking between words

🔊 P4.03

1 We want everyone to be involved in the conversation.
2 There's a lack of consensus in this group at the moment.
3 Did you find writing down your thoughts a good idea?
4 We should focus on ways of building consensus.
5 Think about group needs, not individual needs.
6 Everybody's opinion is of equal weight and is to be respected.
7 Well done everybody! It looks like everyone agrees.
8 No one in the group is more important than anyone else.
9 We can be much more efficient if we work in small groups.
10 The problem is that one or two people always dominate.

## 5.1 Numbers of syllables in words

🔊 P5.01

1 cashier, creating, patience
2 precise, quality, social
3 features, fuel, uses
4 dependable, necessarily, unprecedented
5 planned, prepared, received
6 delivered, innovative, studying
7 cafeteria, opportunity, ultimately
8 fewer, ideas, styles
9 accurate, clients, people

🔊 P5.02

1 I'll prob'ly have a salad.
2 In gen'ral, restaurants are using more technology.
3 They might not hear your order c'rrectly.
4 Some people prefer a bit more social int'raction.
5 I acshly think the quality's better.
6 It's faster than a tradishnal restaurant.
7 They're using really pow'ful technology.
8 Look it up in your diction'ry.

## 5.2 Contrastive stress

🔊 P5.03

1 He's already spent two hours in meetings and an hour writing emails.
2 He should be testing video games but he hasn't even looked at one today.
3 He looked for office jobs, but then a friend mentioned the games-testing job.
4 He applied for the job for a laugh, and was surprised when he got it.
5 When he got the job, his parents often asked, 'Have you found a real job yet?'

**6** After three years in his first job, he left for a position with better pay.

**7** When the company went out of business, he had to find a new job.

**8** The money isn't great, but it's adequate.

## 6.2 Phrasing and pausing

🔊 P6.01

In today's competitive retail industry, security systems have to be more subtle and cost effective. However, they mustn't be so aggressive that it makes potential customers feel uncomfortable and lose the shop sales. Theft prevention has to stop thieves but mustn't frighten real shoppers. With radio frequency ID chips, it is now possible to follow items and send instant alerts to security guards when these are moving towards the door. The retailer also needs to accept that theft is sometimes committed by staff. The solution doesn't need to be expensive or frightening for employees. Staff lockers with glass doors is one simple option.

## 6.4 Stress in phrases

🔊 P6.02

**1** dealing with conflict

**2** currently on vacation

**3** see it from both sides

**4** What do you suggest?

**5** How do we proceed?

🔊 P6.03

**1** that's fine with me, remain calm, management team

**2** tone of voice, review the situation, come to an agreement

**3** at the end of the week, look at the problem, currently on vacation

## 7.2 Unstressed syllables at the end of a sentence

🔊 P7.01

**1** How can I help you, Angela?

**2** I can't hear you very well.

**3** My internet connection isn't working.

**4** I forgot to pay my mobile phone bill for last month.

🔊 P7.02

**1 A:** It might work if you switch it off and back on again.
   **B:** I've already tried switching it off and back on again.

**2 A:** Have you raised this issue with your boss before?
   **B:** This is actually the third time I've raised it.

**3 A:** You need to press the red button.
   **B:** I can't see a red button.

**4 A:** Can I ask you for your phone number, please?
   **B:** But I've already told you what my phone number is.

## 7.4 Introducing a topic

🔊 P7.03

**1** in today's meeting

**2** another way

**3** the first thing we need to do

**4** according to the manager

**5** what we want to do

🔊 P7.04

**1** In today's meeting, we're going to brainstorm how to capture ideas.

**2** Another way is to use your smartphone.

**3** The first thing we need to do is to offer a good service.

**4** According to the manager, we all have good ideas.

**5** What we want to do is make sure that we really think through the issues.

🔊 P7.05

**1 A:** What's on the agenda for today?
   **B:** In today's meeting, we're going to brainstorm how to capture ideas.

**2 A:** How else can you do it?
   **B:** Another way is to use your smartphone.

**3 A:** What should our priority be?
   **B:** The first thing we need to do is to offer a good service.

**4 A:** Who has good ideas?
   **B:** According to the manager, we all have good ideas.

**5 A:** What do we want to do?
   **B:** What we want to do is make sure that we really think through the issues.

## 8.2 Conditional sentences

🔊 P8.01

**1** If we held our meetings in a café, they'd feel less formal.

**2** If she kept her office door open, she'd be easier to talk to.

**3** If I wasn't so busy all the time, I'd get more work done!

**4** They'd probably get more work done if they didn't chat so much.

**5** If I were CEO, I'd give everyone a private office.

**6** You'd know your colleagues better if you talked to them more.

**7** Employees would be more productive if they had private offices to work in.

**8** If you turned off your phone at six o'clock every night, your kids would be happier!

## 8.5 Contractions in speech

🔊 P8.02

**1** I won't be at work tomorrow, so I can't help you.

**2** I couldn't understand the instructions and I didn't know what to do.

**3** The office furniture doesn't look very attractive but it'll be OK for another year.

**4** It seems that the problem's been solved.

**5** The order hadn't been checked.

**6** The company's been taken over.

**7** You mustn't forget to update the stock records.

**8** I'd like to make some recommendations, if you've got time to meet.

🔊 P8.03

**1 A:** There haven't been any problems, have there?
   **B:** Well, there have been a few, actually.

**2 A:** Why didn't you just follow the instructions?
   **B:** I've told you, I couldn't understand them.

**3 A:** We've heard that the company's been taken over.
   **B:** The company has not been taken over!

**4 A:** I hope the report'll be ready tomorrow.
   **B:** Don't worry, it will be.

# Notes